OXFORD BOOKWORMS LIBRARY
Classics

Far from the Madding Crowd

Stage 5 (1800 headwords)

Series Editor: Jennifer Bassett
Founder Editor: Tricia Hedge
Activities Editors: Jennifer Bassett and Alison Baxter

FAR FROM THE

MADDING CROWD

First published in 1874, this novel was an immediate bestseller. The story takes place in the fields and farms of the quiet English countryside, when harvests were gathered by hand, when carts were pulled by horses, and when people's lives followed the pattern of the changing seasons.

That quiet rural world has long since gone, of course, but the passions that coloured that world have not changed. Within the everlasting cycle of seed-time and harvest, love burns as fiercely, as uncontrollably, as ever.

The beautiful Bathsheba Everdene has her own farm and does not need to marry. But she cannot fight off love for ever. There is the shepherd Gabriel Oak, whose love for Bathsheba is quiet and steady. There is Farmer Boldwood, a serious, middle-aged man, who has never been in love before. And there is Sergeant Troy, a handsome young soldier in his bright red coat . . . Bathsheba is self-confident and independent, but she has much to learn about the violent passions of love.

THOMAS HARDY

Far from the Madding Crowd

Retold by
Clare West

OXFORD UNIVERSITY PRESS

OXFORD
UNIVERSITY PRESS

Great Clarendon Street, Oxford OX2 6DP

Oxford University Press is a department of the University of Oxford.
It furthers the University's objective of excellence in research, scholarship,
and education by publishing worldwide in

Oxford New York

Auckland Cape Town Dar es Salaam Hong Kong Karachi
Kuala Lumpur Madrid Melbourne Mexico City Nairobi
New Delhi Shanghai Taipei Toronto

With offices in

Argentina Austria Brazil Chile Czech Republic France Greece
Guatemala Hungary Italy Japan Poland Portugal Singapore
South Korea Switzerland Thailand Turkey Ukraine Vietnam

OXFORD and OXFORD ENGLISH are registered trade marks of
Oxford University Press in the UK and in certain other countries

ISBN 978 0 19 479223 3

A complete recording of this Bookworms edition of
Far From The Madding Crowd is available on audio CD ISBN 978 0 19 479204 2

Printed in China

ACKNOWLEDGEMENTS
Illustrated by: Ron Tiner

Word count (main text): 24,490 words

For more information on the Oxford Bookworms Library,
visit www.oup.com/bookworms

CONTENTS

PEOPLE IN THIS STORY

Bathsheba Everdene
Mrs Hurst, *her aunt*
Liddy, *Bathsheba's maid*
Maryann, *the cleaning-woman in Bathsheba's house*
Benjy Pennyways, *Bathsheba's farm manager*
Gabriel Oak, *a shepherd*
Farmer William Boldwood, *the owner of a large farm
    in Weatherbury*
Sergeant Frank Troy, *a soldier*
Fanny Robin, *a maidservant*

The maltster, *in Weatherbury village*
Jacob Smallbury, *the maltster's son*
Billy Smallbury, *Jacob's son*
Joseph Poorgrass ⎫
Jan Coggan   ⎬ *villagers in Weatherbury*
Laban Tall   ⎭

1

Gabriel Oak falls in love

 Gabriel Oak was a sensible man of good character, who had been brought up by his father as a shepherd, and then managed to save enough money to rent his own farm on Norcombe Hill, in Dorset. He was twenty-eight, a tall, well-built man, who did not seem, however, to think his appearance was very important.

One winter morning he was in one of his fields on the side of Norcombe Hill. Looking over his gate, Gabriel could see a yellow cart, loaded with furniture and plants, coming up the road. Right on top of the pile sat a handsome young woman. As Gabriel was watching, the cart stopped at the top of the hill, and the driver climbed down to go back and fetch something that had fallen off.

The girl sat quietly in the sunshine for a few minutes. Then she picked up a parcel lying next to her, and looked round to see if the driver was coming back. There was no sign of him. She unwrapped the parcel, and took out the mirror it contained. The sun shone on her lovely face and hair. Although it was December, she looked almost summery, sitting there in her bright red jacket with the fresh green plants around her. She looked at herself in the mirror and smiled, thinking that only the birds could see her. But behind the gate Gabriel Oak was watching too.

'She must be rather vain,' he thought. 'She doesn't need to look in that mirror at all!'

As the girl smiled and blushed at herself, she seemed to be dreaming, dreaming perhaps of men's hearts won and lost. When she heard the driver's footsteps, she packed the mirror away. The cart moved on downhill to the toll-gate. Gabriel followed on foot. As he came closer

1

he could hear the driver arguing with the gatekeeper.

'My mistress's niece, that's her on top of the furniture, is not going to pay you the extra twopence,' said the driver. 'She says she's offered you quite enough already.'

'Well, if she doesn't pay the toll, your mistress's niece can't pass through the gate,' replied the gatekeeper.

Gabriel thought that twopence did not seem worth bothering about, so he stepped forward. 'Here,' he said, handing the coins to the gatekeeper, 'let the young woman pass.'

The girl in the red jacket looked carelessly down at Gabriel, and told her man to drive on, without even thanking the farmer. Gabriel and the gatekeeper watched the cart move away. 'That's a lovely young woman,' said the gatekeeper.

'But she has her faults,' answered Gabriel.

'True, farmer.'

'And the greatest of them is what it always is with women.'

'Wanting to win the argument every time? Oh, you're right.'

'No, her great fault is that she's vain.'

A few days later, at nearly midnight on the longest night of the year, Gabriel Oak could be heard playing his flute on Norcombe Hill. The sky was so clear and the stars so visible that the earth could almost be seen turning. In that cold, hard air the sweet notes of the flute rang out. The music came from a little hut on wheels, standing in the corner of a field. Shepherds' huts like this are used as a shelter during the winter and spring, when shepherds have to stay out all night in the fields, looking after very young lambs.

Gabriel's two hundred and fifty sheep were not yet paid for. He knew that, in order to make a success of the farming business, he had to make sure they produced a large number of healthy lambs. So he was determined to spend as many nights as necessary in the fields, to save his lambs from dying of cold or hunger.

The hut was warm and quite comfortable inside. There was a stove, and some bread and beer on a shelf. On each side of the hut was a round hole like a window, which could be closed with a piece of wood. These air-holes were usually kept open when the stove was burning, because too much smoke in a small, airless hut could kill the shepherd.

From time to time the sound of the flute stopped, and Gabriel came out of his hut to check his sheep. Whenever he discovered a half-dead new lamb, he brought the creature into the hut. In front of the stove it soon came back to life, and then he could return it to its mother.

He noticed a light further down the hill. It came from a wooden hut at the edge of a field. He walked down to it and put his eye to a hole in the wood. Inside, two women were feeding a sick cow. One of the women was middle-aged. The other was young and wore a cloak. Gabriel could not see her face.

'I think she'll be all right now, aunt,' said the younger woman. 'I can come and feed her again in the morning. What a pity I lost my hat on the way here!' Just then the girl dropped her cloak, and her long hair fell on to the shoulders of her red jacket. Gabriel recognized the girl of the yellow cart and the mirror, the girl who owed him twopence.

The women left the hut, and Gabriel returned to his sheep.

As the sun was rising the next morning, Gabriel waited outside his hut until he saw the young woman riding up the hill. She was sitting sideways on the horse in the usual lady's position. He suddenly thought of the hat she had lost, searched for it, and found it among some leaves on the ground. He was just going to go up to her to give it back, when the girl did something very strange. Riding under the low branches of a tree, she dropped backwards flat on the horse's back, with her feet on its shoulders. Then, first looking round to make sure no one was watching, she sat up straight again and pulled her dress to her knees, with her legs on either side of the horse. This was obviously easier for riding, but not very ladylike. Gabriel was surprised and amused by her behaviour. He waited until she returned from her aunt's hut, and stepped out into the path in front of her.

'I found a hat,' Gabriel said.

'I found a hat,' he said.

'It's mine,' she said. She put it on and smiled. 'It flew away.'

'At one o'clock this morning?'

'Well, yes. I needed my hat this morning. I had to ride to the hut in that field, where there's a sick cow belonging to my aunt.'

'Yes, I know. I saw you.'

'Where?' she asked, horrified.

'Riding all the way up the hill, along the path,' said Gabriel, thinking of her unladylike position on the horse's back.

A deep blush spread from her head to her neck. Gabriel turned sympathetically away, wondering when he dared look at her again. When he turned back, she had gone.

Five mornings and evenings passed. The young woman came regularly to take care of the sick cow, but never spoke to Gabriel. He felt very sorry he had offended her so much by telling her he had seen her when she thought she was alone.

Then, one freezing night, Gabriel returned, exhausted, to his hut. The warm air from the stove made him sleepy, and he forgot to open one of the air-holes before going to sleep. The next thing he knew was that the girl with the lovely face was with him in the hut, holding his head in her arms.

'Whatever is happening?' he asked, only half-conscious.

'Nothing now,' she answered, 'but you could have died in this hut of yours.'

'Yes, I suppose I could,' said Gabriel. He was hoping he could stay there, close to her, for a long time. He wanted to tell her so, but he knew he could not express himself well, so he stayed silent. 'How did you find me?' he asked in the end.

'Oh, I heard your dog scratching at the door, so I came to see what the matter was. I opened the door, and found you unconscious. It must have been the smoke from the stove.'

'I believe you saved my life, Miss – I don't know your name.'

'There's no need to know it. I probably won't see you again.'

'My name is Gabriel Oak.'

'Mine isn't. You sound very proud of your name.'

'Well, it's the only one I shall ever have.'

'I don't like mine.'

'I should think you'll soon get a new one.'

'Well! That's my business, Gabriel Oak.'

'I'm not very clever at talking, miss, but I want to thank you. Come, give me your hand!'

She hesitated, then offered her hand. He took it, but held it for only a moment. 'I'm sorry,' he said. 'I didn't mean to let your hand go so quickly.'

'You may have it again then. Here it is.'

Gabriel held it longer this time. 'How soft it is, even in winter, not rough at all!' he said.

'There, that's long enough,' she said, but without pulling it away. 'But I suppose you're thinking you'd like to kiss it? You may if you want to.'

'I wasn't thinking any such thing,' said Gabriel, 'but —'

'Oh no you won't!' She pulled her hand sharply away. 'Now discover my name,' she added, laughing, and left.

2

Disaster for Gabriel Oak

 Young Farmer Oak was in love. He waited for the girl's regular visits to the sick cow just as impatiently as his dog waited to be fed. He discovered that her name was Bathsheba Everdene, and that she lived with her aunt, Mrs Hurst. His head was so full of her that he could think of nothing else.

'I'll make her my wife,' he declared to himself, 'or I'll never be able to concentrate on work again!'

When she stopped coming to feed the sick cow, he had to find a reason for visiting her. So he took a young lamb, whose mother had died, and carried it in a basket across the fields to Mrs Hurst's house.

'I've brought a lamb for Miss Everdene,' he told Bathsheba's aunt. 'Girls usually like looking after lambs.'

'Thank you, Mr Oak,' replied Mrs Hurst, 'but Bathsheba is only a visitor here. I don't know if she'll keep it.'

'To tell you the truth, Mrs Hurst, the lamb isn't my real reason for coming. I want to ask Miss Everdene if she'd like to be married.'

'Really?' asked Mrs Hurst, looking closely at him.

'Yes. Because if she would, I'd like to marry her. Do you know if she has any other young men courting her at the moment?'

'Oh yes, a *lot* of young men,' said Mrs Hurst. 'You see, Farmer Oak, she's so handsome, and so well-educated too. Of course, I haven't actually seen any of her young men, but she must have at least ten or twelve!'

'That's unfortunate,' said Farmer Oak, staring sadly at the floor. 'I'm just a very ordinary man, and my only chance was being the first to ask to marry her. Well, that was all I came for. I'd better go home now, Mrs Hurst.'

He had gone halfway across the first field when he heard a cry behind him. He turned, and saw a girl running after him. It was Bathsheba. Gabriel blushed.

'Farmer Oak,' she called breathlessly, 'I want to say – my aunt made a mistake when she told you I had a lot of young men courting me. In fact, I haven't got any, and I've never had any.'

'I *am* glad to hear that!' said Gabriel, with a wide smile, holding out his hand to take hers. But she pulled her hand away quickly. 'I have a nice comfortable little farm,' he added, a little less confidently. 'And when we are married, I'm sure I can work twice as hard as I do now, and earn more.'

He stretched out his arm towards her. Bathsheba moved rapidly behind a tree to avoid him. 'But, Farmer Oak,' she said in surprise, 'I never said I was going to marry you.'

'Well!' said Gabriel, disappointed. 'To run after me like this, and then say you don't want me!'

'I only wanted to explain that my aunt was wrong,' she answered eagerly. 'Anyway, I had to run to catch up with you, so I didn't have time to decide whether I wanted to marry or not.'

'Just think for a minute or two,' replied Gabriel hopefully. 'I'll wait à while, Miss Everdene. Will you marry me? Do, Bathsheba. I love you very much!'

'I'll try to think,' she answered. 'Give me time,' and she looked away from him at the distant hills.

'I can make you happy,' he said to the back of her head. 'You shall have a piano, and I'll practise the flute to play with you in the evenings.'

'Yes, I'd like that.'

'And at home by the fire, whenever you look up, there I'll be, and whenever I look up, there you'll be.'

'Wait, let me think!' She was silent for a while, and then turned to him. 'No,' she said, 'I don't want to marry you. It'd be nice to have a wedding, but having a husband – well, he'd always be there. As you say, whenever I looked up, there he'd be.'

'Of course he would – it would be me.'

'That's the problem. I wouldn't mind being a bride, if I could be one without having a husband. But as a woman can't be a bride alone, I won't marry, at least not yet.'

'What a silly thing for a girl to say!' cried Gabriel. And then he said softly, 'But darling, think again!' He moved round the tree to reach her. 'Why won't you have me?'

'Because I don't love you,' she replied, moving away.

'But *I* love *you* – and I'm happy to be liked, if that's all you feel for me.' He spoke more seriously than he had ever spoken before. 'Only one thing is certain in this life – I shall love you, and want you, and *keep on wanting you* until I die.' His feelings were plain to see in his honest face, and his large brown hands were trembling.

'It seems wrong not to accept you when you feel so strongly,' she replied unhappily. 'I wish I hadn't run after you! But we wouldn't be happy together, Mr Oak. I'm too independent. I need a husband who can keep me in order, and I'm sure you wouldn't be able to do that.'

Gabriel looked hopelessly away and did not reply.

'And, Mr Oak,' she continued in a clear voice, 'I'm so poor that my aunt has to provide a home for me. You're just starting your farming business. It would be much more sensible for you to marry a woman with money. Then you could buy more sheep and improve your farm.'

'That's just what I'd been thinking!' answered Gabriel in surprise.

What common sense she had, he thought admiringly.

'Well then, why did you ask to marry me?' she said angrily.

'I can't do what I think would be – sensible. I must do what my heart tells me.' He did not see the trap she had set for him.

'Now you've confessed that marrying me wouldn't be sensible, Mr Oak. Do you think I'll marry you after that?'

'Don't mistake my meaning like that,' he cried, 'just because I'm honest enough to tell you the truth! I know you'd be a good wife for me. You speak like a lady, everyone says so, and your uncle at Weatherbury has a large farm, I've heard. May I visit you in the evenings, or will you come for a walk with me on Sundays? You don't have to decide at once.'

'No, no, I cannot. Don't insist, don't. I don't love you, so it would be foolish,' she said with a laugh.

No man likes to see his feelings laughed at, so Gabriel Oak said, turning away, 'Very well, then I won't ask you again.'

Gabriel did not see Bathsheba again and two days later he heard that she had left the area, and was now in Weatherbury, a village twenty miles away. Her departure did not stop Gabriel from loving her. In fact he loved her even more deeply now that they were apart.

The next night, before going to bed, Gabriel called his two dogs to come into the house for the night. His old dog, George, obeyed the call, but the younger one was missing. Gabriel was having difficulty training this young dog, which, although enthusiastic, still did not understand a sheep dog's duties. He did not worry about the dog's absence, but went to bed.

Very early in the morning he was woken by the sound of sheep bells, ringing violently. Shepherds know every sound that sheep bells make, and Gabriel immediately realized that his sheep were running fast. He jumped out of bed, threw on his clothes and ran up Norcombe Hill, to his fields near the chalk-pit.

There were his fifty sheep with their lambs, all safe, in one field. But in the other field, the two hundred pregnant sheep had completely disappeared. He noticed a broken gate, and felt sure the sheep had gone through it. There was no sign of them in the next field, but ahead of him at the top of the hill he saw the young dog, looking black against the morning sky. It was standing quite still, staring down into the chalk-pit.

Gabriel felt sick as he realized the horrible truth. He hurried up the hill to the edge of the chalk-pit, and looked down into it. In the deep pit lay his dead and dying sheep, two hundred of them, which would have produced two hundred more in the next few weeks. The young, untrained dog must have chased them up to the edge of the pit, where they fell to their death.

His first feeling was pity for those gentle sheep and their unborn lambs. Then he thought of himself. All his savings, which he had worked so hard for in the last ten years, had been spent on renting the farm. Now his hopes of being an independent farmer were destroyed. He covered his face with his hands.

After a while he looked up. 'Thank God I'm not married to Bathsheba,' he thought. 'What would she have done, married to a husband as poor as I shall be!'

The young dog was shot the next day. Gabriel sold all his farm tools to pay what he owed for the sheep. He was no longer a farmer, just an ordinary man who owned the clothes he was wearing and nothing more. Now he had to find work where he could, on other men's farms.

3

The fire

 Two months later Gabriel went to the great fair at Casterbridge, hoping to find a job as farm manager. But when he realized by late afternoon that none of the farmers at Casterbridge wanted a farm manager, or even a shepherd, he decided to try his luck at another fair the next day. It was fifteen miles further away, in a village the other side of Weatherbury. The name Weatherbury reminded him of Bathsheba, and he wondered if she still lived there. He set out on foot as it was getting dark, and had already walked three or four miles when he saw a cart, half-full of hay, by the side of the road. 'That's a comfortable place to sleep,' he thought, and he was so tired after his long, disappointing day at the fair that when he climbed into the cart, he fell asleep immediately.

A couple of hours later, however, he was woken by the movement of the cart. It was being driven towards Weatherbury by two farm workers, who had not noticed Gabriel. He listened to their conversation.

'She's a handsome woman, that's true,' said one, 'but proud too! And very vain, that's what people say!'

'Oh, if she's vain, Billy Smallbury, I'll never be able to look at her! I'm such a shy man, as you know!' said the other. 'A single woman, and vain! And does she pay her farm workers well?'

'I don't know about that, Joseph Poorgrass.'

Gabriel thought they could be talking about Bathsheba, except that the woman they were discussing seemed to be the mistress of a farm. As the cart was now quite near Weatherbury, Gabriel jumped out, unseen by the two men. He climbed a gate into a field, intending to sleep for the rest of the night under a hay-rick, but then he noticed an unusual light in the darkness, about half a mile away. Something was on fire.

He hurried across the fields towards the fire. Soon, in the rich orange light of the flames, he could see a hay-rick burning fiercely. It was too late to save the rick, so for a few minutes he stood and stared at the flames. But when the smoke cleared for a moment, he was horrified to see, very close to the burning rick, a whole row of wheat-ricks. These probably contained most of the wheat produced on the farm that year, and could catch fire at any moment.

As he rushed towards the wheat-rick that was most in danger, he saw he was not alone. A crowd of farm workers had seen the fire and run into the field to help save the wheat, but they were so confused they did not know what to do. Gabriel took control and gave orders.

'Get a large cloth!' he shouted. 'Put it over the wheat-rick, so the wind can't blow the flames from the hay-rick on to it! Now, you, stand here with a bucket of water and keep the cloth wet!' The men hurried to obey him. The flames, prevented from burning the bottom and sides of the wheat-rick, began to attack its roof.

'Get me a ladder!' cried Gabriel. 'And a branch, and some water!' He climbed up the wheat-rick and sat on the top, beating down the flames with the branch. Billy Smallbury, one of the men who had been in the cart, climbed up with a bucket of water, to throw water on Gabriel and keep the flames off him. The smoke was at its thickest at this corner of the rick, but Gabriel never stopped his work.

On the ground the villagers were doing what they could to stop the fire, which was not much. A little further away was a young woman who had just arrived on her horse, with her maid on foot. They were watching the fire and discussing Gabriel.

'He's a fine young man, ma'am,' said Liddy, the maid. 'And look at his clothes! They're all burnt!'

'Who does he work for?' asked the woman in a clear voice.

'I don't know, ma'am, nor do the others. He's a stranger.'

'Jan Coggan!' called the woman to one of her workers. 'Do you think the wheat is safe now?'

Gabriel climbed up the wheat-rick.

'I think so, yes, ma'am,' he answered. 'If the fire had spread to this wheat-rick, all the other ricks would have caught fire too. That brave young man up there on top of the rick is the one who's saved your wheat.'

'He does work hard,' said the young woman, looking up at Gabriel, who had not noticed her. 'I wish he worked for me.'

As the ricks were no longer in danger, Gabriel started to climb down, and at the bottom he met the maid.

'I have a message from the farmer, who wishes to thank you for all you've done,' she said.

'Where is he?' asked Gabriel, suddenly aware of the chance of getting some work.

'It isn't a he, it's a she,' answered the girl.

'A *woman* farmer?' asked Gabriel.

'Yes, and a rich one too!' said a villager who was standing near. 'She inherited her uncle's farm, when he died suddenly. She has business in every bank in Casterbridge!'

'She's over there, wrapped in a cloak, on her horse,' added the maid. In the darkness Gabriel could only see the shape of a woman sitting on a horse. He walked over to her. Although his face was black from the smoke and his clothes were burnt by the fire, he remembered to lift his hat politely, and asked, looking up at her, 'Do you want a shepherd, ma'am?' She let her cloak fall back from her head in surprise. Gabriel and his cold-hearted darling, Bathsheba Everdene, stared at each other. She did not speak. He only repeated sadly, 'Do you want a shepherd, ma'am?'

Bathsheba turned away into the shadows to consider. She was a little sorry for him, but also glad that she had improved her position since they last met. She realized she had almost forgotten his offer of marriage on Norcombe Hill.

'Yes,' she answered quietly, blushing a little, 'I do want a shepherd. But —'

'He's just the right man, ma'am,' said one of the villagers.

'That's right!' said a second, and a third.

'Then will you men tell him to speak to the farm manager?' said Bathsheba in a businesslike way, as she rode off.

Gabriel soon arranged the details of his employment with Bathsheba's farm manager, Benjy Pennyways, and walked on to the village to find a place to live. As he walked, he thought of Bathsheba. How quickly the young girl he remembered had become the capable mistress of a farm!

When he passed the churchyard, and the ancient trees around it, he noticed that someone was standing behind one of the trees.

'Is this the right way to Weatherbury?' asked Gabriel.

'Oh yes, straight on,' said a girl's voice, low and sweet. After a pause she added, 'You're not a Weatherbury man?'

'No, I'm the new shepherd, just arrived.'

'Only a shepherd! You seem almost like a farmer to me.'

'Only a shepherd,' repeated Gabriel in a dull voice, thinking of the disaster that had destroyed his hopes of being a farmer.

'Please don't tell anyone in the village that you've seen me,' begged the girl. 'I'm rather poor, and I don't want anyone to know about me.' Her thin arms trembled in the cold.

'I won't tell anyone,' said Gabriel, 'but you ought to be wearing a cloak on a night like this.'

'Oh, it doesn't matter. Please go on and leave me.'

He hesitated. 'Perhaps you'd accept this. It's not much, but it's all I have to spare.' He put a coin into her small hand, and as he touched her wrist he noticed how quickly the blood was beating. It was the same quick, hard beat that he felt in his lambs when they were close to death.

'What's the matter? Can't I help you?' he asked. He felt a deep sadness in this thin, weak creature.

'No, no! Don't tell anyone you've seen me! Good night!' She stayed in the shadows, and Gabriel went on to Weatherbury.

4

Fanny Robin disappears

 The farm manager had advised Gabriel to go straight to the malthouse in Weatherbury, to ask for somewhere to stay. That was the place where the men of the village spent their evenings, drinking beer and talking by the fire. When Gabriel entered the warm, dark room, some of Bathsheba's workers recognized him.

'Come in, shepherd, you're welcome,' said one.

'Gabriel Oak is my name, neighbours.'

The ancient maltster, with his white hair and long white beard, turned his old head stiffly towards Gabriel. 'Gabriel Oak of Norcombe!' he said. 'I knew your grandparents well! My boy Jacob and his young son Billy know your family too.' His boy Jacob was bald and toothless, and young Billy was about forty.

'You must be very old, maltster,' said Gabriel politely, 'to have such an old son as Jacob here.'

'Yes, I've lived for over a hundred years,' replied the little old man proudly. 'Sit down and drink with us, shepherd.'

The cup of warm beer passed round the circle of drinkers. There was silence for a moment. Then Gabriel turned the conversation to the matter closest to his heart.

'What kind of mistress is Miss Everdene?' he asked.

'We know almost nothing of her, shepherd,' answered Jan Coggan, a big, cheerful man with a red face. 'She only arrived here a few days ago, when her uncle died. But the Everdenes are a good family to work for. Of course, it's the farm manager who'll be giving us our orders.'

'Ah!' said the maltster, frowning. 'Benjy Pennyways!'

'You can't trust him!' added Jacob darkly.

Soon afterwards Gabriel left with Jan Coggan, who had offered the shepherd a bed in his house. The remaining men were just preparing to leave when suddenly a young man called Laban Tall rushed into the malthouse, almost too excited to speak.

'It's Benjy Pennyways!' he cried. 'Miss Everdene's caught him stealing wheat from the barn! She's sent him away! And worse than that – Fanny Robin, you know, Miss Everdene's youngest maid, is missing! The mistress wants us to look for her tomorrow. And Billy Smallbury, she wants you to go to Casterbridge, to see if you can find the young soldier who's been courting Fanny.'

That night the news spread fast round the village, but did not reach Gabriel, whose dreams were only of Bathsheba. Through the long slow hours of darkness he saw her lovely face and forgot that she did not love him.

The next morning Bathsheba and her maid Liddy were dusting some books, when a visitor arrived at the front door. It was Mr Boldwood, who had a large farm in Weatherbury.

'I can't see him like this, Liddy!' said Bathsheba, looking in horror at her dusty dress. 'Go down and tell him I'm busy.'

When Liddy came back, after Mr Boldwood had gone, Bathsheba asked, 'What did he want, Liddy? And who is he, exactly?'

'He just wanted to ask if Fanny had been found, miss. You know, as she had no family or friends, he was kind enough to pay for her to go to school, and found her a job here with your uncle. He's your neighbour. His farm is next to yours.'

'Is he married? And how old is he?'

'He isn't married. He's about forty, very handsome – and rich. All the girls in the area have tried to persuade him to marry. But he just doesn't seem interested in women. Have *you* ever had an offer of marriage, miss?'

'Yes, I have, Liddy,' answered Bathsheba after a pause, thinking of Gabriel. 'But he wasn't quite good enough for me.'

'Oh, how nice to be able to refuse, when most of us are glad to accept the first offer! And did you love him, miss?'

'Oh no. But I rather liked him.'

In the afternoon Bathsheba called her workers together, and spoke to them in the old hall of the farmhouse.

'Men, I want to tell you that I'm not going to employ a new farm manager. I shall manage the farm myself.' There were gasps of surprise from the men. She gave her orders for the next week's farm work and then turned to one of the men. 'Billy Smallbury, what have you discovered about Fanny Robin?'

'I think she's run away with her young man, ma'am. The soldiers have left Casterbridge, and I suppose she's gone with them.'

'Well, perhaps we'll discover more later. One of you can go and tell Mr Boldwood what Billy says. Now, men, I hope I can trust you all to do your work well for me. Goodnight.'

Later that evening, in a town many miles north of Weatherbury, a small white shape could be seen walking slowly along a path beside a large building. It was a dull, snowy night, with heavy grey clouds hanging low in the sky, the kind of night when hopes are destroyed and love is lost.

'One. Two. Three. Four. Five.' The white shape was counting windows in the building. Then it began to throw small stones, covered in snow, at the fifth window. At last the window opened, and a man called out, 'Who's there?'

'Is that Sergeant Troy?' asked a girl's voice.

'Yes,' answered the man. 'Who are you?'

'Oh Frank, don't you know me?' cried the girl desperately. 'I'm your – I'm Fanny Robin.'

'Fanny!' gasped the man in surprise. 'How did you get here?'

'I walked most of the way from Weatherbury. But, Frank, are you glad to see me? Frank, when will it be?'

'What are you talking about?'

'You know, you promised. When shall we be married, Frank?'

'Oh, I see. Well – you need proper clothes – we must inform the vicar. It takes time. I didn't expect you to come so soon.'

'Oh Frank, I love you so! And – you said you'd marry me —'

'Don't cry now! It's foolish. If I said so, of course I will. I'll come and see you tomorrow to decide the details.'

'Oh yes, Frank, do! I'm staying at Mrs Twill's in North Street. Come tomorrow, Frank! Goodnight, Frank!'

5

Bathsheba sends a valentine

When Bathsheba first appeared at the weekly Casterbridge market, where farmers bought and sold their wheat and animals, she caused a sensation. Men's heads turned to look at her, the only woman there. Like any woman, she was happy to be admired, but she was also determined to sell her wheat at a good price, and to do business with the other farmers like a man. There was one farmer, however, who did not seem to notice her, and this annoyed her a little. It was Mr Boldwood.

One Sunday afternoon, on the thirteenth of February, Bathsheba and Liddy were in the sitting-room together. It was a dull, cold day, and they were both very bored.

'Have you ever tried to discover who you're going to marry, miss,' asked Liddy, 'with a Bible and a key?'

'I don't believe in such foolish games, Liddy.'

'Well, some people believe it works.'

'All right, let's try it,' said Bathsheba suddenly, jumping up from her seat. Together they opened the big family Bible and put a key on a page.

'Now you think of someone you could marry, miss,' said Liddy, 'then read aloud the words on that page, and if the Bible moves, perhaps you'll marry him.'

Bathsheba read the words, holding the Bible. As they watched, the Bible turned in her hands, and Bathsheba blushed.

'Who were you thinking of?' asked Liddy curiously.

'I'm not going to tell you,' answered her mistress.

'By the way, did you notice Mr Boldwood in church this morning?' asked Liddy, making it very clear who *she* was thinking of. 'He didn't turn his head once to look at you!'

'Why should he?' replied Bathsheba, annoyed. 'I didn't ask him to look at me.'

'Oh no. But everybody else in church was looking at you.'

Bathsheba did not reply to this. After a few minutes she said, 'Oh, I nearly forgot the valentine card I bought yesterday!'

'A valentine! Who's it for, miss? Farmer Boldwood?'

'No, of course not. It's for one of the village children, that sweet little boy of Jan Coggan's. I'll write the address on the envelope now, and we'll post it today.'

'What fun it would be to send it to that silly old Boldwood!' laughed Liddy.

Bathsheba paused to consider. It was certainly a little depressing that the wealthiest and most important man in the area did not seem to admire her, as all the other men did.

'We'll throw a coin to decide,' she said lightly. 'No, we shouldn't play with money on a Sunday. I know, we'll throw this book. If it comes down open, I'll send the valentine to Jan's son. If it comes down shut, I'll send it to Boldwood.' The little book went up in the air and came down shut. Bathsheba immediately picked up her pen and wrote Boldwood's address on the envelope.

'Now we need a seal,' she said. 'Look for an interesting one, Liddy. Ah, let's use this one. I can't remember what it says, but I know it's funny.' When she had sealed the envelope, Bathsheba looked closely at the words left by the seal:

'MARRY ME'.

'Just right!' she cried. 'That would make even a vicar laugh!' And so the valentine was sent, not for love, but as a joke. Bathsheba had no idea of the effect it would have.

It arrived at Mr Boldwood's house on the morning of St Valentine's Day, 14th February. He was puzzled, but strangely excited by it. He had never received one before, and all day he thought about it. Who could the woman be, who admired him so much that she sent him a valentine? He kept on looking at it, until the words on the large red seal danced in front of his tired eyes, and he could no longer read them. But he knew what they said:

'MARRY ME'.

The valentine had destroyed the peaceful routine of Boldwood's life. That night he dreamed of the unknown woman, and when he woke up very early, the first thing he saw was the valentine, with its message in red, on the table by his bed.

'Marry me,' he repeated to himself. He was too restless to sleep any more so he went out for a walk. He watched the sun rise over the snowy fields, and on his way home he met the postman, who handed him a letter. Boldwood took it quickly and opened it, thinking it could be from the sender of the valentine.

'I don't think it's for you, sir,' said the postman. 'I think it's for your shepherd.'

Boldwood looked at the address on the envelope:

To the new shepherd,
Weatherbury Farm,
Near Casterbridge.

'Oh, what a mistake! It isn't mine, or my shepherd's. It must be for Miss Everdene's shepherd. His name is Gabriel Oak.'

At that moment he noticed a figure in a distant field.

'Ah, there he is now,' Boldwood added. 'I'll take the letter to him myself.' The shepherd started walking towards the malthouse, and Boldwood followed him, holding the letter.

6

Fanny's mistake

At the malthouse the men were discussing Bathsheba.

'How's she getting on without a farm manager?' the old maltster asked the younger men.

'She can't manage the farm alone,' replied Jacob, 'and she won't listen to our advice. Proud, she is. I've often said it.'

'You have, Jacob, you have, that's true,' agreed little Joseph Poorgrass.

'But she's intelligent,' said Billy Smallbury, 'and must have some common sense.'

'It seems her old uncle's furniture wasn't good enough for her,' said the maltster. 'I hear she's bought new beds, chairs and a piano! If she's a farmer, why does she want a piano?'

Just then they heard a heavy footstep outside, and a voice called, 'Neighbours, can I bring a few lambs in there?'

'Of course, shepherd,' they all replied.

Gabriel appeared in the doorway, his cheeks red and his healthy face shining. On his shoulders were four half-dead lambs, which he put down carefully, close to the fire.

'I haven't got a shepherd's hut here, as I used to have at Norcombe,' he explained. 'These new lambs would die if I couldn't keep them warm for a while. It's very kind of you, maltster, to let me bring them in here.'

'We've been talking of the mistress, and her strange behaviour, shepherd,' said the maltster.

'What have you been saying about her?' asked Gabriel sharply, turning to the others. 'I suppose you've been speaking against her?' he added angrily to Joseph Poorgrass.

'No, no, not a word,' said Joseph, trembling and blushing with terror.

'Well, look here, neighbours.' Gabriel, although normally one of the quietest and most gentle men on earth, had suddenly become aggressive. 'The first man I hear saying anything bad about our mistress will receive this in his face,' and he banged his great heavy hand down on the maltster's table.

'Now don't get so angry, shepherd, and sit down!' said Jacob.

'We hear you're a very clever man, shepherd,' added Joseph Poorgrass from behind the maltster's bed, where he had been hiding. 'We all wish we were as clever as you, don't we, neighbours?' There was general agreement.

'I think mistress ought to have made you her farm manager, you're so suitable for the job,' continued Joseph. He could see that Gabriel was no longer angry.

'I don't mind confessing I was hoping to be her farm manager,' said Gabriel in his honest way. 'But Miss Everdene can do as she likes, and she's chosen to manage her own farm – and keep me as an ordinary shepherd only.' He sounded rather depressed, and looked sadly into the fire.

Before anyone could reply, the door opened and Mr Boldwood came in. He greeted them all and handed the letter to Gabriel.

'I opened this by mistake, Oak,' he said, 'but it must be for you. I'm sorry.'

'Oh, it doesn't matter at all,' answered Gabriel, who had no secrets from anyone. He read this letter:

Dear friend,

I don't know your name, but I want to thank you for your kindness to me on the night I left Weatherbury. I'm also returning the money you gave me. I'm happy to say I'm going to marry the young man who has been courting me, Sergeant Troy. As he is a nobleman's son, I know he wouldn't like me to accept a gift from anyone. Please don't tell anyone about my marriage. We intend to surprise Weatherbury by arriving there as husband and wife, very soon. Thank you again.

Fanny Robin.

'You'd better read it, Mr Boldwood,' said Gabriel. 'It's from Fanny Robin. She wants to keep this a secret but I know you're interested in her. I met her on my way to Weatherbury, but I didn't know then who she was.'

When Mr Boldwood had finished reading the letter, he looked very serious. 'Poor Fanny!' he said. 'I don't think this Sergeant Troy will ever marry her. He's clever, and handsome, but he can't be trusted. What a silly girl Fanny is!'

'I'm very sorry to hear that,' said Gabriel.

'By the way, Oak,' said Mr Boldwood quietly, as he and the shepherd left the malthouse together, 'could you tell me whose writing this is?' He showed Gabriel the envelope containing the valentine.

Gabriel looked at it, and said simply, 'Miss Everdene's.' Then he realized that Bathsheba must have written to Mr Boldwood without signing her name, and he looked, puzzled, at the farmer.

Mr Boldwood replied rather too quickly to Gabriel's unspoken question. 'It's quite normal to try to discover who has written the – valentine. That's the – fun of it.' There was no fun at all in his manner. 'Goodbye, Oak,' he added, and walked slowly back to his empty house.

A few days later, in the town north of Weatherbury where the soldiers were staying, a wedding was arranged. As the church clock in the square struck half-past eleven, a handsome young soldier marched into the church and spoke to the vicar. Then he stood still in the centre of the church, waiting for his bride. The church was full of the women and girls who had attended the morning service and had decided to wait to see the wedding. They watched the young man's straight back, whispering among themselves. The soldier waited without moving a muscle. The church clock struck a quarter to twelve, and still the bride did not come. The whispers stopped, and there was silence. The young man stood as stiff and straight as the church columns around him. There was a little quiet laughter from some of the women, but soon they were silent again, waiting for the end.

As the church clock struck twelve, they listened to the heavy notes ringing out from the church tower. The vicar left his position near the soldier, and disappeared into a back room. Every woman in the church was waiting to see the young man's face, and he knew it. At last he turned, and marched bravely back the way he had come, through the rows of smiling women.

When he got outside and crossed the square, he met a girl hurrying towards the church. When she saw him, the anxiety on her face changed to terror.

'Well?' he said, staring coldly at her.

'Oh Frank, I made a mistake! I thought it was the other church, the one near the market, and I waited there till a quarter to twelve, and then I realized my mistake. But it doesn't matter, because we can just as easily get married tomorrow.'

'You're a fool, to play games with me!' he replied angrily.

'So shall we get married tomorrow, Frank?' she asked, not understanding how seriously she had offended him.

'Tomorrow!' he repeated, and laughed. 'I don't want another experience like that for a while, I can promise you!'

'But Frank,' she begged in a trembling voice, 'it wasn't such a terrible

'Dear Frank, when will our wedding be?' Fanny asked.

mistake! Now, dear Frank, when will our wedding be?'

'Ah, when? God knows!' he said, and turning away from her, walked rapidly away.

7

Farmer Boldwood proposes marriage

 On Saturday at Casterbridge market Boldwood saw the woman who was disturbing his dreams. For the first time he turned his head and looked at her. It was in fact the first time in his life that he had looked at any woman. Up to now he had considered women to be distant, almost foreign creatures, who had nothing to do with him. Now he saw Bathsheba's hair, and every detail of her face. He noticed her figure, her dress, and even her feet. She seemed very beautiful to him, and his heart began to move within him. 'And this woman, this lovely young woman, has asked me to marry her!' he thought. As he was watching Bathsheba selling wheat to another farmer, he was filled with jealousy.

All this time Bathsheba was aware of his eyes on her. At last she had made him look at her! But she would have preferred him to admire her from the beginning, without the encouragement of her valentine. She felt sorry she had disturbed the usual calmness of a man she respected, but considered she could not apologize to him without either offending or encouraging him.

Mr Boldwood did not try to speak to her, and returned home to his farm. He was a man of strong feelings, which normally lay hidden deep inside him. Because he was serious, and did not joke with his neighbours, people thought he was cold. But when he loved or hated, it was with his whole heart. If Bathsheba had known how strong the feelings of this dark and silent figure were, she would have blamed herself terribly for her thoughtlessness. But nobody guessed what lay behind his calm appearance.

A few days later Mr Boldwood was looking at Bathsheba's fields, which were next to his own, when he saw her helping Gabriel Oak with the sheep. To Boldwood, Bathsheba shone like the moon on a dark night. His heart, which had never been touched before, was filled completely with his love for her. He decided to go and speak to her.

As he stopped at the gate of the field, Bathsheba looked up and noticed him. Gabriel was watching her face and saw her blush. He immediately thought of the envelope, with the valentine, that Boldwood had shown him, and suspected Bathsheba of encouraging the farmer to fall in love with her.

Boldwood realized they had noticed him, and suddenly felt unsure of himself. He did not know enough about women to discover from Bathsheba's manner whether she wanted to see him or not. And so he did not enter the field, but walked on, past the gate.

Bathsheba, however, knew that he had come to see her, and felt extremely guilty. She promised herself never again to disturb the peace of this man's life. Unfortunately her promise was made too late, as such promises often are.

It was not until the end of May that Boldwood was brave enough to declare his love. He went to Bathsheba's house, where the maids told him their mistress was watching the sheep-washing. Every spring the sheep were washed in a special pool, to keep their wool clean and to get rid of insects on their skin. Boldwood walked across the fields to the pool, where he found the farm workers busily washing the sheep.

Bathsheba was standing near them, and saw Boldwood coming towards her. She moved away, walking beside the river, but she could hear footsteps behind her in the grass, and felt love all around her, like perfume in the air. Boldwood caught up with her.

'Miss Everdene!' he said quietly.

She trembled, turned, and said, 'Good morning.' She had guessed the truth from the way he spoke those two words.

'I feel – almost too much to think,' he said simply. 'My life does not belong to me any more, Miss Everdene, but to you. I've come to propose marriage to you.'

Bathsheba tried not to show any expression on her face.

'I'm now forty-one,' he continued. 'I've never married, or thought I ever would marry. But we all change, and I changed when I saw you. More than anything else, I want you as my wife.'

'I think, Mr Boldwood, that although I respect you very much, I don't feel – enough for you – to accept your proposal.'

'But my life is worthless without you!' he cried, calm no longer. 'I want you – to let me say I love you, again and again!' Bathsheba remained silent. 'I think and hope you care enough for me to listen to what I have to say!' he added.

Bathsheba was about to ask why he should think that, when she remembered the valentine. After all, it was quite natural for him to think she admired him.

'I wish I could court you with beautiful words,' the farmer went on, 'but I can only say I love you madly and want you for my wife. I wouldn't have proposed if you hadn't allowed me to hope.'

'Mr Boldwood, this is difficult for me! I'm afraid I can't marry you. I'm not in love with you! I should never have sent that valentine – forgive me – it was a thoughtless thing to do.'

'No, no, don't say it was thoughtless! Say it was the beginning of a feeling that you would like me. Just consider whether you can accept me as a husband. I know I'm too old for you, but believe me, I'll take more care of you than a younger man would. You'll have nothing to worry about. You'll have everything you want. God only knows how much you mean to me!'

Bathsheba's young heart was full of pity for this sensitive man who had spoken so simply and honestly.

'Don't say it, don't! You feel so much, and I feel nothing,' she replied. 'Don't discuss it any more. I can't think! Oh, I've given you such pain!'

'Tell me that you don't refuse completely. Give me some hope! May I ask you again? May I think of you?'

'God only knows how much you mean to me!' said Mr Boldwood.

'Yes, I suppose so.'

'May I hope you will accept my proposal next time?'

'No, don't hope! I must go now. Give me time to think.'

'Yes, I'll give you time,' he answered gratefully. 'Thank you, I'm happier now.'

'No, please, don't be happier, Mr Boldwood, if happiness only comes from my agreeing! I must think.'

'I'll wait,' he agreed. They turned away from each other, and returned to their separate houses.

8

Bathsheba's sheep in danger

Because Bathsheba was not at all in love with Farmer Boldwood, she was able to consider his proposal of marriage calmly. It was an offer which many women of good family in the area would have been delighted to accept. He was serious, respectable and rich. If she had wanted a husband, she could not have found a good reason for refusing to marry him. But she was still enjoying her new position as mistress of a farm and house, and although she respected and liked him, she did not want to marry him. However she was honest enough to feel that, as she had begun the courting by sending him the valentine, she ought not to refuse him now.

There was only one person whose opinion she trusted more than her own, and that person was Gabriel Oak. So the next day she decided to ask his advice. She found him with Jan Coggan, sharpening the shears which would be used to shear the sheep.

'Jan, go and help Joseph with the horses,' she ordered. 'I'll help you, Gabriel. I want to talk to you.'

The shears were sharpened on a stone which was turned by a wheel, which was itself turned by a handle. Bathsheba could not manage the handle, so she held the shears while Gabriel turned the handle. 'You aren't holding them right, miss,' he told her. 'Let me show you how.' He let go of the handle, and put his large hands round hers, to hold the shears. 'Like that,' he said, continuing to hold her hands for a peculiarly long time.

'That's enough,' said Bathsheba. 'I don't want my hands held! Turn the handle!' They went on sharpening the shears.

'Gabriel, what do the men think about me and Mr Boldwood?'

'They say you'll marry him before the end of the year, miss.'

'What a foolish thing to say! I want you to contradict it, Gabriel.'

'Well, Bathsheba!' said Gabriel, staring at her in surprise.

'Miss Everdene, you mean,' she said.

'Well, if Mr Boldwood really asked you to marry him, I'm not going to contradict that, just to please you.'

'I said I wanted you just to say it wasn't true that I was going to marry him,' she said, less confidently.

'I can say that, if you wish, Miss Everdene. I could also give my opinion of the way you've behaved.'

He continued with his work. Bathsheba knew that he would always give his honest opinion, even if she asked him whether she should marry another man, and there was nobody else she could trust. 'Well, what is your opinion of my behaviour?' she asked.

'No good, respectable woman would behave like that,' he replied. 'You should never have sent him that valentine.'

Bathsheba blushed angrily. 'Luckily I don't care about your opinion! Why do you think I'm not good or respectable, I wonder? Because I didn't agree to marry you, perhaps!'

'Not at all,' said Gabriel quietly. 'I've long ago stopped thinking about that.'

'Or wishing it, I suppose,' she said, expecting him to protest that he still loved her.

'Or wishing it,' repeated Gabriel calmly.

Bathsheba would not have minded being spoken to angrily by Gabriel for her thoughtlessness, if only he had told her he loved her. But his cold words of blame annoyed her greatly.

'I cannot allow any man to accuse me of bad behaviour!' she cried. 'So you will leave the farm at the end of the week!'

'All right, I will,' said Gabriel calmly. 'In fact I would rather go at once.'

'Go at once then!' she replied angrily. 'Don't let me see your face any more.'

Gabriel put his hands round Bathsheba's, to hold the shears.

'Very well, Miss Everdene.' And so he took his shears and walked quietly away.

It was only twenty-four hours after Gabriel had left the farm that three men came running to report a disaster to Bathsheba.

'Sixty of your sheep —' said Joseph Poorgrass, breathless.

'Have broken through the gate —' said Billy, also breathless.

'And got into a field of young clover!' said Laban Tall.

'They're eating the clover, and they're all swollen up!'

'They'll all die if someone doesn't do something!'

'Oh you fools!' cried Bathsheba. 'Go straight to the field and get them out!'

She rushed towards the clover field, followed by the men. Her sheep were all lying down, their stomachs badly swollen. Joseph, Billy and Laban carried the sheep back into their own field, where the poor creatures lay helplessly without moving.

'Oh, what can I do, what can I do?' cried Bathsheba.

'There's only one way of saving them,' said Laban.

'Someone must make a hole in the sheep's side,' explained Billy, 'with a special tool. Then the air comes out, and the sheep will survive.'

'Can you do it? Can I do it?' she asked wildly.

'No, ma'am. If it isn't done very carefully, the sheep will die. Most shepherds can't even do it.'

'Only one man in the area can do it,' said Joseph.

'Who is he? Let's get him!' said his mistress.

'It's Gabriel Oak. Ah, he's a clever man!' replied Joseph.

'That's right, he certainly is,' agreed the other two.

'How dare you say his name to me!' she said angrily. 'What about Farmer Boldwood? Perhaps he can do it?'

'No, ma'am,' answered Laban. 'When his sheep ate some clover the other day, and were swollen just like these, he sent for Gabriel at once, and Gabriel saved their lives.'

'I don't care! Don't just stand there! Go and find someone!' cried

Bathsheba. The men ran off, without any clear idea where they were going, and Bathsheba was left alone with her dying sheep. 'Never will I send for him, never!' she promised herself.

One of the sheep jumped high in the air, fell heavily and did not move. It was dead. Bathsheba knew she must swallow her pride, and called to Laban, who was waiting at the gate.

'Take a horse, and go and find Gabriel,' she ordered. 'Give him a message from me, that he must return at once.'

Bathsheba and her men waited miserably in the field. Several more sheep jumped wildly into the air, their stomachs horribly swollen and their muscles stiff, then died. At last a rider could be seen across the fields. But it was not Gabriel, it was Laban.

'He says he won't come unless you ask him politely,' Laban reported to Bathsheba.

'What!' said the young woman, opening her eyes wide. Joseph Poorgrass hid behind a tree in case she became violent. 'How dare he answer me like that!' Another sheep fell dead. The men looked very serious, and did not offer their opinion. Bathsheba's eyes filled with tears, and she did not try to hide her anger and her injured pride.

'Don't cry about it, miss,' suggested Billy sympathetically. 'Why not ask Gabriel in a gentler way? I'm sure he'll come then.'

'Oh, he's cruel to me!' said Bathsheba, drying her eyes. 'But I'll beg him, yes, I'll have to!' She wrote a few words quickly on a piece of paper, and at the last moment added at the bottom:

Gabriel, do not desert me!

She blushed a little as she wrote this, and gave the letter to Laban, who rode off again to find Gabriel.

When Gabriel arrived, Bathsheba knew from his expression which words in her note had made him come. He went straight to work on the swollen sheep, and managed to save almost all of them. When he had finished, Bathsheba came to speak to him.

'Gabriel, will you stay on with me?' she asked, smiling.

'I will,' said Gabriel. And she smiled at him again.

A few days later the sheep-shearing began. The sheep were shorn every year at the beginning of June, and their wool was sold. The shearing was always done in the great barn, which had stood on the farm for four centuries. Today the sunshine poured in on the shearers. Bathsheba was watching them carefully to make sure that the sheep were not injured, and that all the wool was cut off. Gabriel was the most experienced shearer. He loved being watched by Bathsheba, and

'Oh Gabriel!' Bathsheba said. 'Be more careful!'

felt warm with pride when she congratulated him on his speed.

But he was not happy for long. Farmer Boldwood arrived at the door of the barn, and spoke to Bathsheba. They stepped outside into the bright sunlight to carry on their conversation. Gabriel could not hear what they were saying, but noticed that Bathsheba was blushing. He continued shearing, feeling suddenly very sad. Bathsheba went back to the house, and returned a short while later in her new green riding dress. She and Boldwood were obviously going for a ride together. As Gabriel's concentration was broken for a moment, his shears cut the sheep's skin. Bathsheba, at the door of the barn, noticed the animal jump, and saw the blood.

'Oh Gabriel!' she said. 'Be more careful!' Gabriel knew she was aware that she herself had indirectly caused the poor sheep's wound. But he bravely hid his hurt feelings, and watched Boldwood and Bathsheba ride away, feeling as sure as the other workers that the couple would soon be married.

9

Bathsheba meets a handsome soldier

 Farmers always gave a special supper to the sheep shearers when they had finished their work. This year Bathsheba had ordered her maids to put a long table in the garden, with the top end of the table just inside the house. The farm workers took their seats, and she sat at the top of the table, so that she was with them, but a little apart. There was an empty place at the bottom of the table. At first she asked Gabriel to sit there, but just then Mr Boldwood arrived, apologizing for his lateness.

'Gabriel,' said Bathsheba, 'will you move again please, and let Mr Boldwood sit there?' Gabriel moved away in silence to another seat. They all ate and drank, and celebrated the end of the sheep-shearing by singing their favourite songs. Mr Boldwood seemed unusually cheerful, and at the end of the meal he left his seat and went to join Bathsheba at her end of the table, just inside the sitting-room. It was growing dark, but Gabriel and the other men could not avoid noticing how Boldwood looked at her. It was clear that the middle-aged farmer was deeply in love.

After a while Bathsheba said goodnight to her farm workers, and closed the sitting-room door and windows. Now she and Boldwood were alone. Kneeling in front of her, he took her hands.

'Tell me, tell me what you've decided!' he begged.

'I'll try to love you,' she answered in a trembling voice. 'And if you think I'll make a good wife, I'll agree to marry you. But, Mr Boldwood, any woman would hesitate before deciding on something as important as marriage. Could you wait a few weeks until I'm sure?'

'I'll be away on business for five or six weeks anyway. Do you really think that by that time you will . . .'

'I feel almost sure that when you come back, at harvest time, I'll be able to promise to marry you. But, remember, I can't promise yet.'

'I don't ask for anything more. I can wait. Goodnight, Miss Everdene!' And he left her.

Bathsheba now realized how thoughtlessly she had behaved towards him, and understood how deeply he loved her. She was very sorry for her mistake and was therefore punishing herself by agreeing to marry him.

That evening she went round the farm as usual, lighting her lamp whenever necessary, to check that all the animals were safe. On her way back, she was walking along the narrow public path which led to her house. It was very dark there, among the trees, and she was a little surprised to hear some footsteps coming towards her. It was unfortunate that she would meet the traveller at the darkest point of the path. As she was about to pass the dark shape, something seemed to attach her skirt to the ground, and she had to stop.

'What's happened? Have I hurt you, friend?' a man asked.

'No,' said Bathsheba, trying to pull her skirt away.

'Ah! You're a lady! The spur on my boot has got tied up with your dress. Have you got a lamp? I'll light it for you.'

The light from the lamp shone suddenly on a handsome young man in a bright red and gold army uniform. He looked admiringly at Bathsheba.

'Thank you for letting me see such a beautiful face!' he said.

'I didn't want to show it to you,' she said coldly, blushing. 'Please undo your spur quickly!' He bent down to pull rather lazily at his boots. 'You are making it even worse,' she accused him angrily, 'to keep me here longer!'

'Oh no, surely not,' smiled the soldier. 'Don't be angry. I was doing it so that I could have the pleasure of apologizing to such a lovely woman.'

Bathsheba had no idea what to say. She wondered whether to escape

'I've never seen a woman as beautiful as you,' said the young man.

by pulling the material away, but did not want to tear her best dress.

'I've seen many women in my life,' continued the young man, staring into her face, 'but I've never seen a woman as beautiful as you. I don't care if you're offended, that's the truth.'

'Who are you, then, if you don't care who you offend?'

'People know me in Weatherbury. My name's Sergeant Troy. Ah, you see, your skirt's free now! I wish you and I had been tied together for ever!'

She pulled her dress quickly away from his spurs, and ran up the path and into her house. The next day she discovered from Liddy that Sergeant Troy's supposed father was a doctor, but people said his real father was a nobleman. He had been brought up in Weatherbury, and was well known as a young soldier with a great interest in girls. Bathsheba could not remain angry for long with someone who admired her as much as he obviously did. It was unfortunate that Boldwood, when courting her, had forgotten to tell her, even once, that she was beautiful.

Sergeant Troy was certainly an unusual man. He lived only in the present, caring nothing for the past or the future. Because he never expected anything, he was never disappointed. To men he usually told the truth, but to women, never. He was intelligent and well-educated, and proud of his success with women.

A week or two after the sheep-shearing, Bathsheba was in the hayfields, where her workers were cutting the hay. She was surprised to see a bright red figure appear from behind a cart. Sergeant Troy had come to help on the farm. She blushed as the young soldier came to speak to her.

'Miss Everdene!' he said. 'I didn't realize it was the "Queen of Casterbridge market" I was speaking to the other night. I apologize for expressing my feelings so strongly to you then. Of course, I'm not a stranger here. I often helped your uncle on the farm, and now I'm helping you.'

'I suppose I must thank you for that,' replied the Queen of Casterbridge market rather ungratefully.

'You're cross because I was honest when I spoke to you that night. But I couldn't look at you, and say you aren't beautiful!'

'You are pretending, Sergeant Troy!' said Bathsheba, laughing in spite of herself at his clever way of talking.

'No, Miss Everdene, you must let me say how lovely you are! What's wrong with that?'

'It's wrong because – it isn't true,' she said, hesitating.

'But you know that everybody notices how beautiful you are, don't you?'

'Well, no – that is, I've heard Liddy say they do, but . . .' She paused. She had never intended to become involved in this kind of conversation with the soldier, but somehow he had trapped her into replying. 'Thank you for helping the men with the hay,' she continued. 'But please don't speak to me again.'

'Oh Miss Bathsheba! That's too hard! I won't be here long. I'm going back to the army in a month.'

'But you don't really care about a word from me, do you?'

'I do, Miss Everdene. Perhaps you think it's foolish of me to want just a "good morning", but you have never loved a beautiful woman like yourself, as I do.'

'But you only saw me the other night! I don't believe you could fall in love so fast. I won't listen to you any more. I wish I knew what time it was. I've spent too much time with you.'

'Haven't you got a watch, miss? I'll give you one,' and he handed her a heavy gold watch. 'That watch belonged to a nobleman, my father, and is all the inheritance I have.'

'But Sergeant Troy, I can't take this! It's your father's, and so valuable!' said Bathsheba, horrified.

'I loved my father, true, but I love you more.' The young man was not pretending now, as he looked at Bathsheba's beautiful, excited face.

'Can it be true, that you love me? You have seen so little of me! Please take it back!'

'Well then, I'll take it,' he said, 'because it's all I have to prove that I come of good family. But will you speak to me while I'm in Weatherbury? Will you let me work in your fields?'

'Yes! Or no, I don't know! Oh, why did you come and disturb me like this!'

'Perhaps, in setting a trap, I've caught myself. Such things sometimes happen. Goodbye, Miss Everdene!'

Blushing and almost crying, Bathsheba hurried home, whispering to herself, 'Oh what have I done? What does it mean? I wish I knew how much of what he says is true!'

10

Bathsheba in love

 Once or twice during the next few days Bathsheba saw Troy working in her hayfields. He behaved in a pleasant, friendly manner towards her, and she began to lose her fear of him.

'Cutting your hay is harder work than sword practice!' he told her one day, a smile lighting up his handsome face.

'Is it? I've never seen sword practice,' she answered.

'Ah! Would you like to?' asked Troy.

Bathsheba hesitated. She had heard wonderful stories from people who had watched soldiers practising, stories of shining metal flashing through the air.

'I would like to see it, very much.'

'Well, I'll show you. I can get a sword by this evening. Will you . . .' and he bent over her, whispering in her ear.

'Oh no!' said Bathsheba, blushing. 'I couldn't.'

'Surely you could? Nobody would know.'

'Well, if I came, Liddy would have to come with me.'

'I don't see why you want to bring her,' Troy said coldly.

'Well then, I won't bring her – and I'll come. But only for a very short time.'

So at eight o'clock that evening, Bathsheba found herself, in spite of her doubts, climbing the hill near her house and going down the other side. Now she was in what seemed like a natural theatre, a deep, round hollow in the ground. It was completely hidden from her house and the path. This was the place where Troy had asked her to meet him.

And Troy, in his bright red uniform, was there.

'Now,' he said, producing his sword, which flashed in the evening sunlight, 'let me show you. One, two, three, four. Like this! A sword can kill a man in a second.'

Bathsheba saw a kind of rainbow in the air, and gasped.

'How cruel and murderous!' she cried.

'Yes. Now I'll pretend to fight you. You are my enemy, but the only difference from a real fight is that I'll miss you each time. Stand in front of me, and don't move!'

Bathsheba was beginning to enjoy this. 'I'll just test you first,' added Troy, 'to see whether you're brave enough.'

The sword flashed in the air, from her left to right side. It seemed to go through her body. But there it was again in Troy's hand, perfectly clean and free from blood.

'Oh!' she cried, frightened. 'Have you killed me? No, you haven't! How did you do it?'

'I haven't touched you,' said Troy quietly. 'Now, you aren't afraid, are you? I promise I won't hurt you, or even touch you.'

'I don't think I'm afraid. Is the sword very sharp?'

'Oh no – just stand very still. Now!'

In a second, Bathsheba could no longer see the sky or the ground. The shining weapon flashed above, around and in front of her, catching light from the low sun and whistling as it rushed through the air. Never had Sergeant Troy managed his sword better than today.

'Your hair is a little untidy,' he said. 'Allow me,' and before she could move or speak, a curl dropped to the ground. 'You are very brave, for a woman!' he congratulated her.

'It was because I didn't expect it. Now I'm afraid of you, I am, really!'

'This time I won't even touch your hair. I'm going to kill that insect on your dress. Stand still!'

Not daring to tremble, she saw the point of his sword coming towards her heart, and, sure that this time she would die, closed her

A curl of Bathsheba's hair dropped to the ground.

eyes. But when she opened them, she saw the insect, dead, on the point of the sword.

'It's magic!' she cried. 'And how could you cut off one of my curls with a sword that isn't sharp?'

'It's sharper than any knife,' he said. 'I had to lie to you about that, to give you the confidence to stand still.'

Bathsheba's feelings were almost too much for her to control, and she sat down suddenly in the grass.

'I could have died,' she whispered.

'You were perfectly safe,' Troy told her. 'My sword never makes a mistake. I must leave you now. I'll keep this to remind me of you.' He bent to pick up the curl of hair, which he put carefully in his pocket, next to his heart. She was not strong enough to say or do anything. He came closer, bent again, and a minute later his red coat disappeared through the grass. Bathsheba blushed guiltily and tears rolled down her face. In that minute Troy had kissed her on the lips.

Determined, independent women often show their weakness when they fall in love, and Bathsheba had very little experience of the world, or of men. It was as difficult for her to see Troy's bad qualities, which he kept carefully hidden, as to admire Gabriel Oak's good ones, which were not all obvious at first sight.

One evening a few days later, Gabriel went to find his mistress. He knew that she was falling in love, and had decided to warn her of the mistake she was making. He found her walking along a path through the fields.

'I was worried about your walking alone, miss,' he said. 'It's rather late, and there are some bad men in the area.' He was hoping to introduce Troy's name as one of the 'bad men'.

'I never meet any,' said Bathsheba lightly.

Gabriel tried again. 'Farmer Boldwood will be taking care of you in future, of course.'

'What do you mean, Gabriel?'

'Well, when you and he are married, miss, as everybody expects. You've let him court you, after all.'

'Everybody is wrong, Gabriel. I didn't promise him anything. I respect him, but I won't marry him.'

'I wish you had never met that young Sergeant Troy, miss,' he said sadly. 'He's not good enough for you.'

'How dare you say that! He's of good family, and well-educated!' replied Bathsheba angrily.

'He can't be trusted, miss. Don't trust him, I beg you.'

'He's as good as anybody in the village! He goes to church regularly! He told me so himself.'

'I'm afraid nobody has ever seen him in church. I certainly haven't.' Gabriel's heart ached when he saw how completely Bathsheba trusted the soldier.

'That's because he enters by the old tower door and sits at the back, where he can't be seen,' she replied eagerly.

'You know, mistress,' said Gabriel in a deep voice full of sadness, 'that I love you and shall love you for ever. I accept that I can't marry you now that I'm poor. But Bathsheba, dear mistress, think of your position! Be careful of your behaviour towards this soldier. Mr Boldwood is sixteen years older than you. Consider how well he would look after you!'

'Leave my farm, Gabriel,' said Bathsheba, her face white with anger. 'You can't speak like that to me, your mistress!'

'Don't be foolish! You've already sent me away once. How would you manage without me? No, although I'd like to have my own farm, I'll stay with you, and you know why.'

'Well, I suppose you can stay if you wish. Will you leave me here now please? I ask not as your mistress, but as a woman.'

'Of course, Miss Everdene,' said Gabriel gently. He was a little surprised by her request, as it was getting dark, and they were on a lonely hill some way from her house. As she moved away from him, the reason became clear. The figure of a soldier appeared on the hill and came to meet Bathsheba. Gabriel turned away and walked sadly home. On his way he passed the church, where he looked closely at the old tower door. It was covered with climbing plants, and clearly had not been used for years.

Half an hour later Bathsheba arrived home, with Troy's words of love still in her ears. He had kissed her a second time. Wild and feverish with excitement, she sat down immediately to write to Boldwood, to inform him that she could not marry him. The letter would reach him on his business trip. She was so eager to send the letter at once that she called Liddy to post it.

'Liddy, tell me,' she said urgently, when her maid entered the room, 'promise me that Sergeant Troy isn't a bad man. Promise me that he doesn't chase girls, as people say!'

'But, miss, how can I say he doesn't if he —'

'Don't be so cruel, Liddy! Say you don't believe he's bad!'

'I don't know what to say, miss,' said Liddy, beginning to cry. 'I'll make you angry whatever I say!'

'Oh, how weak I am! How I wish I'd never seen him! You see how much I love him, Liddy! Don't tell anyone my secret, Liddy!'

'I'll keep your secret, miss,' said Liddy gently.

11

Farmer Boldwood becomes desperate

 Liddy was allowed a week's holiday to visit her sister, who lived a few miles away. To avoid seeing Mr Boldwood, Bathsheba herself arranged to visit Liddy at her sister's home for a day or two. She left her cleaning-woman, Maryann, in charge of the house, and set out on foot one evening.

She had walked only about two miles when she saw, coming towards her, the one man who she did not wish to see. His changed appearance showed her that he had received her letter.

'Oh, is it you, Mr Boldwood?' she said, with a guilty blush.

'You know how I feel about you,' he said slowly. 'A love as strong as death. A letter cannot change that feeling.'

'Don't speak of it,' she whispered.

'Then I have nothing to say. Your letter was excellently clear. We are not going to marry.'

Bathsheba said confusedly, 'Good evening,' and walked on a little further. But Boldwood could not let her go.

'Bathsheba – darling – is it really final?'

'Indeed it is.'

'Oh Bathsheba, have pity on me! I am mad with love for you! Don't refuse me now! You turned to me, and encouraged me, before I ever thought of you!'

'What you call encouragement was a childish joke. I'm deeply sorry I sent the valentine. Must you go on reminding me of it?'

'I love you too much to blame you for it! Bathsheba, you are the first woman I have ever loved. How nearly you promised to marry me! What has happened to your kindness towards me?'

Bathsheba looked him quietly and openly in the face and said, 'Mr

Boldwood, I promised you nothing.'

'How can you be so heartless! If I had known how awfully bitter this love would be, I'd have avoided you, and been deaf to you! I tell you all this, but what do you care!'

Bathsheba's control was breaking. She shook her head desperately as the man's angry words rained down on her.

'Forgive me, sir! I can't love as you can!'

'That's not a good reason, Miss Everdene! You aren't the cold woman you're pretending to be! You're hiding the fact that you've a burning heart like mine. Your love is given to another man!'

He knows! she thought. He knows about Frank!

'Why didn't Troy leave my darling alone?' he continued fiercely. 'Tell me honestly, if you hadn't met him, would you have accepted my proposal?'

She delayed her answer, but she was too honest to stay silent. 'Yes,' she whispered.

'In my absence he stole my most valuable prize from me. Now I've lost my respect and my good name, and everybody laughs at me. Marry him, go on, marry him! I would have died for you, but you have given yourself to a worthless man. Perhaps he has even kissed you! Tell me he hasn't!'

She was frightened of Boldwood's anger, but she answered bravely, 'He has. I'm not ashamed to speak the truth.'

'I would have given a fortune to touch your hand,' cried Boldwood wildly, 'but you have let a man like that – kiss you! One day he'll be sorry, and realize the pain he's caused me!'

'Be kind to him, sir,' she cried miserably, 'because I love him so much!'

Boldwood was no longer listening to her. 'I'll punish him! Sweet Bathsheba, forgive me! I've been blaming you, but it's his fault. He stole your dear heart away with his lies. When I find him, I'll fight him! Keep him away from me, Bathsheba!'

The desperate man stood still for a moment, then turned and left her. Bathsheba walked up and down, crying and whispering to herself, then threw herself down by the road, exhausted. She knew that Troy was away in Bath at the moment, but would be returning to Weatherbury very soon. If he came to visit her, and Boldwood saw him, a fierce argument would be the result, and Troy could be hurt. But perhaps Gabriel and Boldwood were right, and she should not see him again? If she could only see Troy now, he would help her to decide! She jumped to her feet, and hurried back along the road to Weatherbury.

That night Maryann, the only person sleeping in Bathsheba's house, was woken by strange noises in the field where the horses were kept. She looked out of her bedroom window just in time to see a dark figure leading Bathsheba's horse and cart out of the field. She ran to Jan Coggan's house for help. Jan and Gabriel immediately rode after the thief. After riding for some time in the dark, they finally caught up with the cart at a toll-gate.

'Keep the gate closed!' shouted Gabriel to the gatekeeper. 'That man's stolen the horse and cart!'

'What man?' asked the gatekeeper, puzzled.

Gabriel looked closely at the driver of the cart, and saw a woman – Bathsheba. She turned her face away from the light when she heard his voice, but Jan Coggan had also recognized her. She was quick to hide her surprise but not her annoyance.

'Well, Gabriel,' she asked coldly, 'where are you going?'

'We thought someone had stolen the horse and cart.'

'How foolish of you! Some important business made me change my plans. I'm on my way to Bath. I may visit Liddy at her sister's later. I arrived home during the night, so I didn't wake Maryann up. I just took the horse and cart myself. Thank you for taking all this trouble, but it wasn't necessary.'

The gatekeeper opened the gate and she passed through. Coggan and Gabriel turned their horses and rode slowly home. Gabriel said, 'I think we'll keep this strange trip of hers to Bath a secret, Jan,' and Jan agreed.

So at first the people of Weatherbury had no idea where she had gone. She stayed away for two weeks, and there were reports that she had been seen in Bath with Sergeant Troy. Gabriel knew in his heart that this must be true. He worked as hard as ever on her farm, but all the time there was a deep ache inside him.

12

Bathsheba makes her choice

On the same day that Bathsheba arrived home, Mr Boldwood went to apologize to her for speaking so violently the last time he had seen her. He knew nothing of her trip to Bath, and supposed she had only been to visit Liddy. But at her door he was told he could not see her, and he realized she had not forgiven him.

On his way home through Weatherbury he saw the coach from Bath. It stopped at the usual place, and a soldier in a red and gold uniform jumped down. Sergeant Troy picked up his bag and was about to take the road to Bathsheba's house, when Boldwood stepped forward.

'Sergeant Troy? I am William Boldwood.'

'Indeed?' said Troy, showing little interest.

'I want to speak to you – about two women.'

Troy saw the heavy stick Boldwood was holding, and realized how determined he was. He decided it was worth being polite.

'I'll listen with pleasure, but do speak quietly.'

'Well then, I've heard about your relationship with Fanny Robin, and I think you ought to marry her.'

'I suppose I ought. Indeed, I want to, but I cannot.'

'Why can't you?'

Troy was going to reply immediately, but he stopped himself. 'I am too poor,' he said, looking quickly at Boldwood to see if the farmer believed him. Boldwood did not notice the look.

'I don't want to talk about right or wrong, I just want to discuss business with you. I was engaged to Miss Everdene, when you came and —'

'Not *engaged*,' said Troy.

'More or less engaged,' insisted Boldwood. 'If you hadn't come, she would certainly have accepted my proposal by now. Well, her position in society is so much higher than yours that you can't hope to marry her. So all I ask is that you don't bother her any more, and marry Fanny.'

'Why should I?' asked Troy carelessly.

'I'll pay you. If you leave Weatherbury today, I'll give you fifty pounds. Fanny will have fifty pounds for wedding clothes, and I'll give her five hundred pounds the day she marries you.' Boldwood's manner showed that he was a little ashamed of offering money, but he was prepared to do almost anything to prevent Troy marrying Bathsheba.

Troy appeared to consider the offer. 'It's true I like Fanny best, although she's only a maid. Fifty pounds now, you said?'

'Here's the money,' said Boldwood, handing the soldier a purse of gold coins.

'Stop, listen!' said Troy in a whisper. Light footsteps could be heard on the road, coming from Bathsheba's house. 'It's Bathsheba! She's expecting me. I must go and speak to her, and say goodbye to her, as you and I have arranged.'

'Why do you need to speak to her?'

'She'll look for me if I don't. Don't worry, you'll hear every word I say to her. It may help you in your courting, when I've gone! Stand over there behind the tree, and listen.'

Troy stepped forward and whistled a double note.

'Frank, darling, is that you?' It was Bathsheba's voice.

'Oh God!' said Boldwood, unheard behind the tree.

'Yes, it's me,' replied Troy.

'You're so late, Frank,' she continued. 'The coach arrived a long time ago! Frank, it's so lucky! There's nobody in my house except me tonight, so nobody will know about your visit.'

'Excellent,' said Troy. 'But I'll just have to collect my bag, so you run home and I promise to be there in ten minutes.'

'Yes, Frank.' She ran back to her house.

Troy turned to Boldwood, who had stepped out from behind the tree, his face white and his whole body trembling.

'Shall I tell her I cannot marry her?' laughed the soldier.

'No, no, wait! I have more to say to you!' whispered Boldwood, the muscles in his face strangely out of control.

'Now,' said Troy, 'you see my problem. I can't marry them both. But I have two reasons for choosing Fanny. First, I like her best, I think, and second, you're paying me for it.'

At that moment Boldwood lost control. He attacked Troy fiercely, holding his neck with both hands.

'Wait,' gasped Troy, who had not expected this, 'let me breathe! If you kill me, you injure the woman you love!'

'What do you mean?' cried the farmer. 'I should kill you like a dog!' But he let go of Troy's neck, and listened.

'You heard how Bathsheba loves me and expects me to visit her tonight. Soon the whole village will know this. The only way to save her good name, and her position in Weatherbury, is for me to marry her.'

'True, true,' agreed Boldwood after a pause. 'Troy, marry her! Poor, weak woman! She must love you madly to give herself so completely to you!'

'But what about Fanny?' asked the soldier cleverly.

'I should kill you like a dog!' cried Boldwood.

'Don't desert her, Troy, I beg you! I don't mean Fanny, I'm speaking of Bathsheba! How can I persuade you? I know! I'll pay you five hundred pounds on the day you marry Bathsheba!'

Troy was secretly shocked at Boldwood's wild offer.

'And I'll receive something now as well?' he asked.

'Yes, all the money I have with me!' He counted the coins in his pocket. 'Twenty-one pounds – it's all for you!'

'Give me the money, and we'll go to her house. I'll ask her to marry me. Of course I won't say anything about the money.'

They went along the road to the farmhouse, and Boldwood waited outside while Troy entered. He returned in a moment with a piece cut out of a Bath newspaper.

'Here, read this first,' he said, smiling. And Boldwood read:

MARRIAGES: On the 17th, in Bath, Frank Troy, Sergeant, to Bathsheba Everdene of Weatherbury.

The paper fell from Boldwood's hands, as the soldier began to laugh. 'Fifty pounds to marry Fanny. Twenty-one pounds not to marry Fanny, but Bathsheba. And now you see I'm already Bathsheba's husband. You're a fool, Boldwood. Although I may be a bad man, I'd never bribe anyone to marry, as you've tried to. And Fanny? She left me long ago, and I don't know where she is. I've searched everywhere for her. Now take your money back! I don't want it!' and Troy threw the gold coins into the road.

'You black-hearted dog! I'll punish you one day, remember that!' cried the broken man. Troy laughed loudly as he closed Bathsheba's front door.

Through the whole of the long night that followed, Boldwood's dark figure could be seen walking over the hills of Weatherbury like a ghost.

Just before the clock struck five the next morning, Gabriel and Coggan were walking to the hayfields past their mistress's house, when they saw a surprising sight. Bathsheba's bedroom window was open, and looking out of it was a handsome man, with his red jacket undone. It was Sergeant Troy.

'She's married him!' whispered Coggan. Gabriel said nothing, but he felt so ill that he had to rest on the gate for a moment. He thought with pity of her future, as he knew her marriage to Troy could not be happy for long.

'Good morning, friends!' shouted Troy cheerfully to the men.

'We must be polite to him,' whispered Coggan, 'if he's married the mistress.'

'Good morning, Sergeant Troy,' said Gabriel miserably.

'Now that I've left the army, I'll soon be down in the fields with you again,' said Troy lightly. 'My new position won't change that, and I'll be friendly with you all, just as before. Drink to my health, men.' And he threw a coin towards Gabriel, who refused to pick it up. Coggan, however, put it in his pocket.

As they went on their way, they noticed Mr Boldwood riding past them. Gabriel forgot his own sadness when he saw the bitterness and deep despair on the farmer's face.

13

The storm

There was always a harvest supper for the farm workers after all the hay and wheat had been cut. On behalf of his wife, Sergeant Troy decided to have it one evening at the end of August, in the great barn. The weather was unpleasantly warm that night. On his way to the harvest supper Gabriel stopped to check the eight huge hay- and wheat-ricks. If, as he suspected, there was a storm, the ricks, which were all uncovered, would be badly damaged.

He went on to the barn, where the farm workers had already finished eating and started dancing. Gabriel had to wait until Sergeant Troy had finished his dance with Bathsheba before he could warn him about possible damage to the ricks. Troy, however, was enjoying himself too much to listen to Gabriel's message.

'Friends,' he was saying, 'I've ordered brandy to be served to you all, so that we can celebrate my wedding properly.'

'No, Frank, don't give them brandy,' begged Bathsheba, 'it will only do them harm!'

'Don't be silly!' said Troy. 'Friends, let's send the women home! Then we men can drink and sing as much as we like!' Angrily, Bathsheba left the barn, followed by the other women.

Gabriel left soon afterwards. Later, when he went to check that Bathsheba's sheep were safe, he noticed that they looked very frightened. They were crowded together in a corner, their tails pointing the same way. To the shepherd this meant they were expecting a storm. He went to look at the ricks again. Should the whole harvest of the farm, worth at least seven hundred and fifty pounds, be lost because of a woman's weakness? Never, if I can prevent it! thought Gabriel.

He returned to the barn to ask the other farm workers to help him cover the ricks. But the only noise he could hear coming from the barn was the men's loud and regular breathing, and when he entered, he found them all asleep, including Troy. The brandy, which they had been too polite to refuse, had made them drunk in a very short time, as they were not used to drinking anything stronger than beer. It was useless trying to wake them.

Gabriel left the barn, and returned to the ricks, two of which he managed to cover with the heavy material kept on the farm for this purpose. The only way to cover the other six ricks was by thatching them with straw, and this was a long and difficult job to do alone.

The moon disappeared, and there was a slow, light wind, like the breath of a dying man, as Gabriel climbed the ladder and started thatching high up on top of the third rick. Lightning flashed in the sky, and there was a loud crash of thunder. In the sudden brightness Gabriel could see every tree around him, until the light disappeared just as suddenly, leaving him in the blackest darkness. He knew his position was dangerous, but considered his life was not valuable enough to worry about.

Another flash of lightning allowed him to see the figure of a woman running towards the rick. Was it Bathsheba?

'Is that you, ma'am?' he called to the darkness.

'Who's there?' said Bathsheba's voice.

'It's Gabriel. I'm on the rick, thatching.'

'Oh Gabriel! I'm so worried about the ricks! Can we save them? The thunder woke me. I can't find my husband. Is he there?'

'No, he isn't. He's – asleep in the barn.'

'He promised me the ricks would be covered, and he hasn't done it! Can I help you? Let me help!'

'You can bring the straw up to me in armfuls, if you aren't afraid to climb the ladder in the dark,' said Gabriel.

'I'll do anything to help!' she said. She started to go up and down the ladder, carrying the straw. In the brightness of the lightning Gabriel saw their two shadows, wildly enlarged, on the hill in front of him. Then came the loudest crash so far.

'How terrible!' cried Bathsheba, and held on to his arm. The lightning flashed in a wild dance of death, and thunder came from every part of the huge sky. Bathsheba and Gabriel could only stare, and tremble at the strange and dangerous beauty of the storm.

As they watched, a tall tree in front of them seemed to be burning with a white flame. There was a final, violent crash of thunder, and in the bright light they saw that the tree had been torn in half by the lightning.

'That was close to us!' said Gabriel. 'We'd better go down.' They climbed down and stood together in the darkness, Bathsheba seeming to think only of the storm, Gabriel thinking only of her.

At last he said, 'The storm appears to have passed, but the rain will be coming soon. I'll go up and finish thatching the ricks.'

'Gabriel, you are kind to me! Oh why aren't the others here? Don't tell me, I know. They're all drunk in the barn, aren't they? It was my husband's fault. Gabriel, I want to tell you something.' The soft flashes of the dying lightning showed her face, very white against the black sky. 'I care about your good opinion of me, so I want to explain *why* I went to Bath that night. It wasn't to marry Troy, it was to break off my relationship with him. Perhaps you wonder why I married him then? Well, I suppose I must tell you. It was because he told me he had seen a woman more beautiful than me, and said that if I wanted him as a husband, I must marry him at once! I was wild with love and jealousy, so I married him!' Gabriel did not reply.

'I'll bring some more straw up to you, shall I?' she offered.

She made several more journeys before he noticed her tiredness. 'I think you'd better go indoors now,' he said, as gently as a mother. 'I'll finish the work alone.'

'If I'm useless, I'll go,' said Bathsheba. 'But, oh, if you fell . . .!'

'You aren't useless, but you're tired. You've done well.'

'And you've done better,' she said gratefully. 'Thank you a thousand times, Gabriel! Goodnight.'

She disappeared in the darkness. He went on thatching in a kind of dream. She had spoken more warmly to him tonight than she had ever done when she was unmarried and free to speak as warmly as she liked.

The wind changed and became stronger. At the same time heavy rain started falling. As Gabriel worked on the top of the ricks, he suddenly remembered that, eight months before, he had been fighting against fire in the same place as desperately as he was fighting against water now – and for love of the same woman, who did not love him.

It was not until seven o'clock in the morning that Gabriel climbed down from the last rick, exhausted and wet to the skin. He noticed figures coming out of the barn, walking slowly and painfully to their homes. They all looked ashamed except Troy, who was whistling cheerfully as he entered the farmhouse. None of them thought of looking at the ricks.

On his way back to Coggan's house, Gabriel met Boldwood.

'How are you, sir?' asked Gabriel.

'Yes, it's a wet day. Oh, I'm very well, thank you.'

'You look a little different, sir.'

'No, you're wrong, Oak. I'm just the same. Nothing hurts me. But *you* look tired.'

'I've been working all night to get our ricks covered. Never worked so hard in my life! Yours are safe of course, sir?'

'Oh yes.' Boldwood added after a silence, 'What did you ask?'

'Your ricks are all covered?'

'No, none of them. I forgot to tell the men to thatch them. I expect most of my wheat will be destroyed in this rain.'

'Forgot,' repeated Gabriel to himself. It was difficult to believe that the most careful farmer in the area would lose all his harvest because of a moment's forgetfulness. This would never have happened before Boldwood fell in love with Bathsheba.

Boldwood clearly wanted to talk, although it was still raining heavily. 'Oak, you knew I wanted to get married.'

'I thought my mistress was going to marry you,' said Gabriel sympathetically. 'However, nothing that we expect ever happens.'

He spoke with the calmness of a man used to disaster.

'Perhaps the villagers laugh at me,' said Boldwood with a pretended lightness.

'Oh no, I don't think so.'

'But the truth is that we were never engaged, so she never broke off the engagement, you see.' But Boldwood could not remain calm. 'Oh

Gabriel,' he said wildly, 'I'm weak and foolish, and I feel it's better to die than to live!' After a silence, he continued more normally. 'I've accepted the fact of her refusal now. I'm sorry, of course, but no woman has ever controlled my life. Well, good morning.'

14

Bathsheba discovers the truth

Summer turned into autumn and one Saturday evening in October Bathsheba and her husband were riding home from Casterbridge market.

'Yes, if it hadn't rained so hard, I'd have won two hundred pounds easily, my love,' Troy was saying. 'The horse I put my money on fell over in the mud, you see. Such bad luck!'

'But Frank,' said Bathsheba miserably, 'do you realize you've lost more than a hundred pounds in a month with this awful horse-racing? It's foolish of you to spend my money like that! You'll promise not to go to the next race, on Monday, won't you?'

'It doesn't matter whether I go or not. I've already put money on an excellent horse in the Monday race. Don't cry, Bathsheba! If I'd known you were so cautious, I'd never have —'

He did not finish what he was saying. Just then they noticed a woman walking towards them. Although it was almost dark, they could see that she was poorly dressed.

'Please, sir, do you know what time the Casterbridge workhouse closes?' she asked in a voice of extreme sadness.

Troy jumped in surprise, but kept his face turned away from her before replying, 'I don't know.'

When the woman heard him speak, and looked up to his face, her expression showed both pain and happiness. She gave a cry, and fell to the ground, unconscious.

'Oh poor thing!' cried Bathsheba. 'I'll help her!'

'No, stay on your horse, and take mine!' ordered Troy, jumping down. 'Take the horses to the top of the hill.'

Bathsheba obeyed, and moved away. Troy lifted up the woman.

'I thought you were far away, or dead!' he told her, in a strangely gentle voice. 'Why didn't you write to me, Fanny?'

'I was afraid to.'

'Have you any money? No? Here's all I have, it's not much. I can't ask my wife for any more at the moment.' The woman said nothing. 'Listen,' continued Troy, 'I'll have to leave you now. You're going to the Casterbridge workhouse? Well, stay there for tonight and tomorrow anyway, but I'll find somewhere better for you. I'll meet you on Monday morning at ten o'clock on the bridge just outside town. I'll bring you all the money I can. Goodbye!'

At the top of the hill Bathsheba turned and saw the woman walking slowly on towards Casterbridge. Troy soon caught up with his wife. He looked very upset.

'Who is that woman?' Bathsheba looked closely into his face.

'She's not important to either of us,' he replied coldly.

'I think you know her,' Bathsheba went on.

'I don't care what you think!' he answered, and they continued their ride in silence.

The two miles to Casterbridge seemed a very long way to the woman, who was tired and ill. Sometimes she walked, sometimes she rested a little, beside the road. All through the night her eyes were fixed on the lights of Casterbridge, the end of her journey. At six o'clock the next morning she finally fell in front of the door of the workhouse, and the people there took her in.

Bathsheba and her husband did not speak much that evening, or the following day. But on Sunday evening Troy said suddenly,

'Bathsheba, could you let me have twenty pounds? I need it.'

'Ah!' she said sadly, 'for the races tomorrow. Oh, Frank, only a few weeks ago you said I was far sweeter than all your other pleasures! Now won't you stop risking money on horses, which is more a worry than a pleasure? Say yes to your wife, Frank, say yes!' Her beautiful face would have persuaded most men, including Troy if he had not been married to her, but he no longer loved her enough to agree to anything she wanted.

'Well, the money isn't for racing anyway,' he said. 'Don't keep me short of money, Bathsheba, or you'll be sorry.'

'I'm sorry already,' she replied, 'sorry that our love has come to an end.'

'Love always ends after marriage. I think you hate me.'

'No, not *you*. I only hate your faults.'

'Then why not help me to improve? Come, let's be friends. Just give me the twenty pounds.'

'Well, here's the money. Take it.'

'Thank you. I expect I'll be away before breakfast tomorrow.'

'Must you go, Frank? Stay with me! There was a time when you used to call me darling. Now you don't care how I spend my time.'

'I must go,' said Troy, taking out his watch. He opened the back of the watch case, and Bathsheba, who happened to be looking, saw that there was a curl of hair hidden inside.

'Oh Frank!' she gasped. 'A woman's hair! Whose is it?'

Troy closed the watch immediately and replied carelessly, 'Why, yours of course. I'd quite forgotten I had it.'

'You're lying, Frank. It's yellow hair. Mine is darker.'

'Well, all right, if I must tell you, it's the hair of a young woman I was going to marry before I met you.'

'Tell me her name! Is she married?'

'I can't tell you her name, but she's single.'

'Is she alive? Is she pretty?'

'Yes to both questions.'

'How can she be pretty, poor thing, with hair that colour?'

'Her hair has been admired by everybody who's seen her. It's beautiful hair! Don't be jealous, Bathsheba! You shouldn't have married me if you didn't trust me!'

'This is all I get for loving you so much!' cried Bathsheba bitterly. 'I would have died for you when I married you, and now you laugh at my foolishness in marrying you! But you'll burn that hair, won't you, Frank, to please me?'

Troy only answered, 'I have a duty to someone in my past. Mistakes were made which I must put right. That's more important than my relationship with you. If you're sorry you married me, well, so am I!'

'Frank, I'm only sorry if you love another woman more than me,' said Bathsheba in a trembling voice. 'You like the woman with that pretty hair. Yes, it is pretty! Was she the woman we met on the road last night?'

'Well, yes. Now you know the truth, I hope you're happy.'

'You haven't told me everything. Tell me the whole truth,' she said, looking bravely into his face. 'I never thought I'd beg a man to do anything, but my pride has all gone!'

'Don't be so desperate!' said Troy crossly. He left the room.

Bathsheba was in deep despair. She knew that she had lost her independence as a woman, which she had been so proud of. She hated herself for falling in love so easily with her handsome husband, who, she now realized, could not be trusted.

The next morning Troy left the house early. Bathsheba was walking in her garden, when she noticed Gabriel Oak and Mr Boldwood deep in conversation in the road. They called to Joseph Poorgrass, who was picking apples, and soon he came along the path to Bathsheba's house.

'Well, what's the message, Joseph?' she asked, curious.

'I'm afraid Fanny Robin's dead, ma'am. Dead in the Casterbridge workhouse.'

'No! Why? What did she die from?'

'I don't know, ma'am, but she was never very strong. Mr Boldwood is sending a cart to bring her back to be buried here.'

'Oh, I won't let Mr Boldwood do that! Fanny was my uncle's maid, and mine too. How very sad to die in a workhouse! Tell Mr Boldwood that *you* will drive my new cart over to Casterbridge this afternoon to fetch her body. And Joseph, put flowers on the cart for poor Fanny. How long was she in the workhouse?'

'Only a day, ma'am. She arrived, ill and exhausted, on Sunday morning. She came on foot through Weatherbury.'

The colour left Bathsheba's face at once. 'Along the road from Weatherbury to Casterbridge?' she asked eagerly. 'When did she pass Weatherbury?'

'Last Saturday night it was, ma'am.'

'Thank you, Joseph, you may go.'

Later that afternoon Bathsheba asked Liddy, 'What was the colour of poor Fanny Robin's hair? I only saw her for a day or two.'

'She used to keep it covered, but it was lovely golden hair, ma'am.'

'Her young man was a soldier, wasn't he?'

'Yes, and Mr Troy knows him well.'

'What? Mr Troy told you that?'

'Yes. One day I asked him if he knew Fanny's young man, and he said he knew him as well as he knew himself!'

'That's enough, Liddy!' said Bathsheba, her anxiety making her unusually cross.

15

Fanny's revenge

 That afternoon Joseph Poorgrass was bringing Fanny's coffin back from Casterbridge. Feeling a little frightened of the dead body behind him in the cart, and depressed by the autumn fog, he stopped for some beer at a pub, where he met Jan Coggan and Laban Tall. There Gabriel Oak found the three men, completely drunk, two hours later. As Joseph was clearly incapable of driving the cart, Gabriel drove it to Weatherbury himself. On the way into the village, the vicar stopped him.

'I'm afraid it's too late now for the burial,' he said, 'but I can arrange for the body to be buried tomorrow.'

'I could take the coffin to the church for the night, sir,' offered Gabriel, hoping to prevent Bathsheba from seeing it.

But just then Bathsheba herself appeared. 'No, Gabriel,' she said. 'Poor Fanny must rest in her old home for her last night. Bring the coffin into the house.'

The coffin was carried into a small sitting-room and Gabriel was left alone with it. In spite of all his care, the worst had happened, and Bathsheba was about to make a terrible discovery. But suddenly he had an idea. He looked at the words written simply on the coffin lid – *Fanny Robin and child*. With a cloth Gabriel carefully removed the last two words. Quietly he left the room.

Bathsheba was in a strange mood. She felt lonely and miserable, but she had not stopped loving her husband, in spite of her anxiety about his past. She was waiting for him to come home, when Liddy knocked and entered.

'Ma'am, Maryann has just heard something . . .' she hesitated a little. 'Not about you or us, ma'am. About Fanny. There's a story in

Weatherbury that. . .' Liddy whispered in her mistress's ear.

Bathsheba trembled from head to foot.

'I don't believe it!' she cried. 'There's only one name on the coffin lid! But I suppose it could be true.'

She said no more, and Liddy went quietly out of the room. Bathsheba felt almost sure she knew the truth about Fanny and Troy, but she wanted to be certain. She entered the sitting-room where the coffin lay. Holding her hot hands to her forehead she cried, 'Tell me your secret, Fanny! I hope it isn't true there are two of you! If I could only look at you, I'd know!'

After a pause, she added slowly, '*And I will.*'

A few moments later, she stood beside the uncovered coffin. Staring in, she said, 'It was best to know the worst, and I know it now!' Her tears fell fast beside the dead pair in the coffin, tears for Fanny and for herself. Although Bathsheba, not Fanny, had married Troy, in death

'*You are nothing to me, nothing,*' said Troy.

68

Fanny was the winner. She was taking her revenge now on Bathsheba for the difficulties she had experienced in her life.

Bathsheba forgot the passing of time as she looked at Fanny's cold white face and yellow hair, and did not realize Troy had arrived home. He threw open the door and came in. He did not guess who was in the coffin.

'What's the matter? Who's dead?' he asked.

Bathsheba tried to push past him. 'Let me out!' she cried.

'No, stay, I insist!' He held her arm and together they looked into the coffin.

Troy stood completely still when he saw the mother and baby. Little by little his shoulders bent forward, and his face showed deep sadness. Bathsheba was watching his expression closely, and she had never been more miserable. Slowly Troy knelt to give Fanny Robin a gentle kiss.

Bathsheba threw her arms round his neck, crying wildly from the depths of her heart, 'Don't, don't kiss them! Oh Frank, no! I love you better than she did! Kiss me too, Frank! *You will kiss me too, Frank!*'

Troy looked puzzled for a moment, not expecting this childlike cry from his proud wife. But then he pushed her away.

'I will not kiss you!' he said.

'Can you give me a reason?' asked Bathsheba, fighting to control herself. Perhaps it was unfortunate that she asked.

'I've been a bad, black-hearted man, but this woman, dead as she is, is more to me than you ever were, or are, or can be. I would have married her, if I'd never seen your beautiful face! And I wish I *had* married her!' He turned to Fanny. 'But never mind, darling,' he said, 'in the sight of God you are my wife!'

At these words a long, low cry of despair and anger came from Bathsheba's lips. 'If she's – that, what – am I?'

'You are nothing to me, nothing,' said Troy heartlessly. 'A ceremony in front of a vicar doesn't make a marriage. I don't consider myself your husband.'

Bathsheba wanted only to get away from him and his words. She ran straight out of the house. She stayed out all night, wrapped in a cloak, waiting for the coffin to be taken for burial. As soon as the men had taken it away the next morning, she re-entered the house, very cautiously to avoid Troy, but her husband had gone out very early and did not return.

16

Sergeant Troy leaves

 When Bathsheba ran out of the house the previous night, Troy first replaced the coffin lid, then went upstairs to lie on his bed and wait miserably for the morning.

The day before, on Monday, he had waited for Fanny, as arranged, on the bridge just outside Casterbridge, for over an hour. He had Bathsheba's twenty pounds and seven pounds of his own to give Fanny. When she did not come, he became angry, remembering the last time she had failed to arrive, on her wedding day. In fact she was at that moment being put in her coffin at the workhouse, but he did not know that. He rode straight to the races at Budmouth and stayed there all afternoon. But he was still thinking of Fanny, and he did not risk any money on the horses. Only on his way home did he suddenly realize that illness could have prevented her from meeting him, and only when he entered the farmhouse that evening did he discover that she was dead.

On Tuesday morning Troy got up and, without even thinking about Bathsheba, went straight to the churchyard to find the position of Fanny's grave. He continued on foot to Casterbridge to order the best gravestone available for twenty-seven pounds, which was all the money he had. Having arranged for it to be put on the grave that afternoon, he returned to Weatherbury in the evening, with a basket of flowering plants. The new gravestone was already in place, and he worked solidly for several hours in the churchyard, putting the plants carefully into the soft earth of her grave. When it started raining, however, he decided to spend the rest of the night in the shelter of the church, and finish his planting in the morning.

The rain that night was unusually heavy, and water began to pour from a broken pipe on the church roof straight on to Fanny's grave. As the earth there had only recently been dug, the grave became a kind of muddy pool. Soon the plants were floating on top of the grave, and then were washed away in the stream of water flowing through the churchyard.

When Troy woke up, stiff and still tired, he went out of the church to finish work on the grave. The rain had stopped, and the sun was shining through the red and gold autumn leaves. The air was warm and clear. As Troy walked along the path, he noticed it was very muddy, and covered with plants. Surely these could not be the ones he had planted? He turned the corner and saw the damage the heavy rain had done.

The new gravestone was stained with mud, and there was a shallow hole in the grave, where the water had poured in. Nearly all the plants had been washed out of the grave.

This strange accident had a worse effect on Troy than any of his troubles, worse even than Fanny's death. He had tried to show his love for her, knowing that he had failed to do so when she was alive. Planting the flowers was also a way of softening his feelings of sadness and guilt at her death. And now his work had been destroyed! He was too depressed to start work on the grave again. He left it as it was, and went silently out of the churchyard. A minute later he had left the village.

Meanwhile Bathsheba had spent a day and a night as a willing prisoner in a small bedroom in her house. Except when Liddy brought her food or messages, she kept the bedroom door locked so that her husband could not come in. Liddy knew there was trouble between husband and wife, but did not know the reason. On Wednesday morning she brought breakfast up to Bathsheba.

'What heavy rain we had in the night, ma'am!' she said.

'Yes, and there was a strange noise from the churchyard.'

'Gabriel thinks it was water from a broken pipe on the church roof, and he's gone there to see. Are you going to the churchyard, ma'am, to look at Fanny's grave?'

'Did Mr Troy come in last night?' Bathsheba asked anxiously.

'No, ma'am, he didn't. And Laban Tall says he saw Mr Troy walking out of the village towards Budmouth,' replied Liddy.

Budmouth, thirteen miles away! At once Bathsheba's heart felt lighter. 'Yes, Liddy, I need some fresh air. I'll go to see Fanny's grave,' she said, and after breakfast she walked almost cheerfully to the churchyard.

She saw the hole in the grave and the expensive new gravestone, but did not think it could be Fanny's. She looked round for a plain grave. Then she noticed Gabriel reading the words on the gravestone, and her eyes followed his:

This stone was put up by Francis Troy in loving memory of Fanny Robin, who died on October 9, 1866, aged 20

Gabriel looked anxiously at her to see if she was upset, but she remained calm. She asked him to fill in the hole, and have the broken water pipe repaired. Finally, to show she did not hate the woman who had caused her such bitterness, she replanted the flowers herself, and cleaned the muddy gravestone, so that the words could be read clearly. Then she went home.

Troy, meanwhile, was walking towards the south. He could not decide what to do next. All he knew was that he had to get away from Weatherbury. At the top of a hill he saw the sea, stretching for miles in front of him. Now he felt more cheerful, and decided to swim. So he climbed down the cliffs, undressed on the beach and jumped into the sea. The water was so smooth that he swam confidently out to where it was very deep. Here he was surprised and a little frightened to find that he was being carried further out to sea. He suddenly remembered that the Budmouth coast was famous for the number of swimmers drowned there every year, and he began to be afraid that he would soon be one of them. However strongly he swam, the sea pulled him further away from the coast, and he was already beginning to feel tired and breathless.

Just then he saw a small boat moving out to sea, towards a ship. With his right arm he swam, and with his left he waved wildly, shouting as loudly as he could. The sailors saw him at once, and rowed over to rescue him.

17

Farmer Boldwood begins to hope

 When Troy did not return, Bathsheba felt neither happiness nor sadness. She had no hope for the future. She was sure that one day he would return, and spend the rest of her money. Then they would have to sell the farm. She could do nothing to prevent it.

One Saturday at Casterbridge market, a stranger came up to her. 'I must tell you, ma'am,' he said, 'your husband is dead.'

'No, it can't be true!' gasped Bathsheba. Darkness came over her eyes, and she fell. But not to the ground. Boldwood, who had been standing in a corner watching her, ran forward to catch her.

'Tell me more,' he said to the stranger, as he held the unconscious girl gently in his arms.

'The police found her husband's clothes on the beach. He must have been swimming, and drowned off the Budmouth coast.'

There was a strange excitement in Boldwood's face, but he said nothing. He carried her to a private room at the hotel, where she could rest until she felt well enough to ride home.

When she arrived home, still feeling weak and confused, Liddy had already heard the news. 'Shall we get some black clothes made for you, ma'am?' said the maid, hesitating a little.

'No, Liddy. It isn't necessary. You see, I think he may still be alive. I feel – I think I'm sure he's alive!'

But the following Monday Troy's death was reported in the local newspaper. A witness had seen him in deep water, shouting and waving for help. And when his clothes and his watch, found on the beach, were delivered to the farmhouse, Bathsheba began to doubt that he was alive. She opened the back of his watch case and took out the curl of golden hair.

'He was Fanny's and she was his,' she said to herself. 'They should be together. I mean nothing to either of them. Why should I keep her hair?' She held the curl over the fire. 'No, I won't burn it, I'll keep it in memory of her, poor thing!'

Through the autumn and winter Bathsheba's life was more peaceful. She no longer took such an interest in the farm, and very sensibly appointed Gabriel Oak her farm manager. He had already been doing the job unofficially, and now would be paid for it. At last his good qualities were being recognized. Gabriel's luck had certainly changed. Boldwood could not concentrate on farming these days either. His wheat and hay had all been so damaged by the rain that it was worthless. Weatherbury people were shocked by the changes they had noticed recently in Farmer Boldwood. Soon he himself realized that something must be done, and arranged for Gabriel to manage his farm too. So Gabriel was responsible for both the important farms in the area, while their owners sat alone in their lonely farmhouses.

After a time Boldwood started to hope that one day, if Bathsheba remarried at all, she would marry him. He tried to maintain a friendly, businesslike relationship with her, keeping his love for her out of sight, until the right moment came to propose again. He had no idea how long he would have to wait to marry her, but he was prepared to wait for the rest of his life.

The right moment did not come until the following summer when most of the Weatherbury people attended the great sheep fair at Greenhill. Gabriel was there with Bathsheba's and Boldwood's sheep, and so were both his employers. This year a travelling circus put up its tent and offered the public a horse-riding show. Most of Bathsheba's farm workers were already in the tent, when Bathsheba herself arrived to see the show. At the back of the tent, behind a curtain, were the circus riders, and one of them, pulling on his boots, was Sergeant Troy.

After being rescued, Troy had decided to stay on the ship and work as a sailor, but he was not happy with this travelling life, and finally returned to England. He hesitated to go back to Bathsheba and a comfortable life on the farm. Perhaps Bathsheba would fail at farming and then he would be responsible for her. And anyway, perhaps she would not welcome him back. For the moment he was working as actor and horse-rider with the circus. So it was with no plans for the future that Troy found himself at Greenhill fair, dangerously close to Weatherbury.

When he looked through a hole in the curtain to see the audience, he was horrified to see his wife. She looked more beautiful than he remembered. Perhaps she would laugh at him, a nobleman's son, working in a circus! As he rode into the tent, he was careful to keep his face away from her, and remain wrapped in his cloak. She did not seem to recognize him.

When the show was over, Troy went out into the darkness. In the large tent where meals and drinks were being served, he saw Bathsheba talking to a man. Was she forgetting her husband so soon? thought Troy angrily. He decided to listen to their conversation, and knelt down outside the tent, making a little hole with his knife in the heavy cotton so that he could see the two people inside.

She was drinking a cup of tea, which Boldwood had just brought her. Troy watched her every movement. She was as handsome as ever, and she belonged to him. After a few moments Troy got up and walked slowly from the tent. He was considering what to do next.

Meanwhile Boldwood had offered to ride back to Weatherbury with Bathsheba, as it was getting late, and she accepted. Her pity for the man she had hurt so deeply made her behave more kindly towards him than was perhaps sensible. Her kindness made poor Boldwood dream of their future marriage, and suddenly, unable to stop himself, he said, 'Mrs Troy, will you marry again some day?'

'You forget that my husband's death has never been proved, so I may not really be a widow,' she said, confused. 'I've a feeling he's alive, and I'm not thinking of marrying anyone else.'

'Do you know, Bathsheba, that according to the lawyers, you can remarry seven years after your husband's supposed death, that is, six years from now? Could you – promise to marry me then?'

'I don't know. Six years is too far away. I'm bitterly sorry I behaved so stupidly towards you, but – I can promise I'll never marry another man while you want me to be your wife, but —'

'You could put right the mistake you made by promising to be my wife in six years' time!' There was wild hope in his eyes.

'Oh, what shall I do? I don't love you, but if I can give you happiness by just promising, then I will – consider – and promise – soon. Shall we say, by Christmas?'

'You'll promise at Christmas. Well, I'll say no more.'

As Christmas came nearer, Bathsheba became more anxious, and one day she confessed her difficulty to Gabriel.

'The saddest reason of all for agreeing to his proposal,' she said, 'is that if I don't, I'm afraid he'll go mad. His feelings are so extreme. I don't say that because I'm vain, but I believe I hold that man's future in my hands. Oh Gabriel, it's a terrible worry!'

'Then why don't you promise, ma'am? I don't think people would think it wrong. The only thing that makes it wrong in my view is that you don't love him.'

'That is my punishment, Gabriel, for playing that foolish trick with the valentine on him.' Gabriel had given her a reasonable, sensible answer, as she knew he would, but she felt annoyed with his cool advice. Not once had he spoken of *his* love for her, or said that *he* could wait for her too. She would have refused him of course, but at least it would have shown that he still admired her.

18

Mr Boldwood's Christmas party

For months Weatherbury people had been discussing the party that Mr Boldwood was going to give just before Christmas, and now the day had finally arrived. Bathsheba was getting ready for it.

'I'm upset, Liddy, it's foolish of me, I know,' she said. 'I wish I didn't have to go to the party. I haven't spoken to Mr Boldwood since the autumn, when I promised to see him at Christmas, so I'll have to go. My black silk dress, please.'

'Surely you don't need to wear black tonight, ma'am? You've been a widow for fourteen months now. That's a long time.'

'No, if I wear a bright dress, people will say I'm encouraging Mr Boldwood. How do I look, Liddy?'

'I've hardly ever seen you look so lovely, ma'am.'

'I risk offending him if I don't go. Oh, I wish I could have continued as I've been for the last year or so, with no hopes or fears, and no pleasures and no sadness.'

'If Mr Boldwood asked you to run away with him, what would you say, ma'am?' said Liddy with a smile.

'Now, Liddy, no joking. This is far too serious. I won't marry *anyone* for a long time. Get my cloak. It's time to go.'

At the same time, in his farmhouse, Boldwood was also dressing. He was trying on a new coat which had just been delivered. Tonight he wanted to look his best.

Just then Gabriel entered, to report on farm business.

'Oh, Oak,' said Boldwood. 'You're invited to the party tonight, of course.'

'I'll try to come, if I'm not too busy,' said Gabriel quietly. 'I'm glad to see you looking happier, sir.'

'Yes, I confess I'm cheerful tonight. But my happiness depends on a hope. Oak, my hands are shaking. Could you help me with the buttons on this coat?' And as Gabriel came forward to help, he went on feverishly, 'Oak, does a woman keep her promise to become engaged? You know women better than I do – tell me.'

'I don't think I understand women well at all. But if she wants to put right a mistake, she may keep a promise like that.'

'I think she will,' whispered Boldwood. 'She says she can think of me as a husband seven years after Troy's disappearance.'

'Seven years,' said Gabriel, shaking his head. 'A long time.'

'But it isn't seven years!' answered Boldwood impatiently. 'It's only five years, nine months and a few days now!'

'Don't build your hopes on her promise, sir. Remember, she disappointed you once. And she's young.'

'She never promised me that first time, so she's never broken her promise to me yet. I trust her to keep her word. But let's talk business for a moment, Oak. You work so hard as my farm manager that I want you to have a larger share of the profits. I know a little about your secret. You have warm feelings for her too, but you've let me succeed in courting her! I want to show you how grateful I am for that.'

'Oh, that's not necessary, thank you,' said Gabriel hurriedly. 'I must get used to my disappointment as other men have.' He left, rather worried by Boldwood's strange manner.

Outside the front door of Boldwood's house a group of men were talking quietly.

'Sergeant Troy was seen in Casterbridge this afternoon,' said Billy Smallbury. 'His body was never found, you know, neighbours.'

'Should we tell the mistress?' asked Laban Tall. 'Poor woman! What a mistake she made in marrying him!'

Just then Boldwood came out and walked to the gate. He did not notice the men, who were standing in the darkness.

'I hope to God she'll come!' he whispered. 'Oh, my darling, my darling, why do you make me wait like this!'

They all heard his words clearly. The sound of wheels came from the road, and Bathsheba arrived. Boldwood took her into the house, and the door closed behind them.

'I didn't realize he was still in love with her!' said Billy.

'Poor Mr Boldwood, the news will be hard for him,' said Jan Coggan. 'We'll have to tell the mistress her husband's still alive. We'll go in and find the right moment to speak to her.'

But the right moment never came. Bathsheba had planned to stay at the party for only an hour, and she was in fact preparing to leave when Boldwood found her alone in an upstairs room.

'Mrs Troy, you can't go!' he said wildly. 'We've only just begun!'

'I'd like to go now. I think I'll walk home.'

'You know what I want to say to you?' Bathsheba looked silently at the floor. 'You do give it?' he said eagerly.

'Give what?' she asked, although she knew well what he meant.

'Your promise! Just a business arrangement between two sensible people who no longer think of love. To marry me in five to six years! You owe it to me!'

'I have no feeling in that matter at all,' she replied, hesitating. 'But if I must, I promise – if I'm really a widow.'

'You'll marry me in five and three-quarter years' time?'

'Let me think! I'll marry nobody else. Oh, I don't know! Is Frank really dead? Perhaps I should ask a lawyer!'

'Say the words, my dear one, and I won't speak about it any more. A long engagement, then marriage – Oh Bathsheba! Promise yourself to me!' he begged wildly, forgetting his cool, businesslike manner. 'I've loved you so much and for so long!'

'Very well,' she said after a pause, 'I'll marry you six years from now if we're both alive and if my husband doesn't return.'

'Then wear this ring for me.' Boldwood took from his pocket a diamond engagement ring, and held it out to her.

'No, no, I can't, I don't want anyone to know!'

'Just wear it tonight, to please me!' Bathsheba could say no more, and weakly let him put it on her finger. He left her.

In a few minutes she was calmer. She put on her cloak and went downstairs. She paused at the foot of the stairs. Boldwood was standing near the fire, and he had just noticed that a group of villagers were whispering among themselves.

'What's the matter, men?' he asked cheerfully. 'Is anybody engaged or married, born or dead? Tell us the news, Tall.'

'I wish somebody *was* dead,' replied Laban Tall in a whisper.

'What was that, Tall?' asked Boldwood. 'Speak out, if you have anything to say.'

At that moment there was a knock on the front door. One of the men opened it. 'A stranger wants to see Mrs Troy,' he said.

'Ask him to come in,' said Boldwood.

The message was given, and Troy, wrapped up to his eyes in the cloak, stood in the doorway. Those who knew he was in the area recognized him immediately. Boldwood did not. He said, 'Come in, stranger, and have a Christmas drink with us!'

Troy entered, threw off his cloak and looked Boldwood in the face. But it was only when he laughed that Boldwood recognized the man who had destroyed his hope and happiness once and was about to do it again.

Troy turned to Bathsheba. She had dropped miserably on to the lowest stair. Her mouth was blue and dry, her eyes empty and staring. He said, 'Bathsheba, I've come here for you!' She did not reply. 'Come home with me, do you hear!' He went towards her.

A strange, thin voice, full of despair, came from the fireplace. 'Bathsheba, go with your husband!' said Boldwood.

She did not move, and when Troy stretched out his hand to pull her towards him, she fell back with a quick, low scream.

A second later there was a loud bang, and the hall was filled with smoke. At Bathsheba's cry, Boldwood's despair had turned to anger. From the wall above the fireplace he had taken a gun and shot Troy, who now lay very still. Boldwood turned the gun on himself, but was stopped by one of his men.

'It doesn't matter!' Boldwood gasped. 'There's another way to die!'

He crossed the room to Bathsheba, and kissed her hand. Then he went out into the darkness before anyone could prevent him.

19

Bathsheba and Gabriel

 Gabriel arrived at Boldwood's house about five minutes after the shooting. The villagers were all shocked and silent, but Bathsheba was sitting on the floor, calmly holding Troy's head.

'Gabriel,' she said simply, 'I'm afraid it's too late, but ride to Casterbridge for a doctor. Mr Boldwood has shot my husband.' Gabriel obeyed at once, and while riding along was thinking so hard about the shooting that in the darkness he failed to notice a man walking along the road to Casterbridge. That man was Boldwood, on his way to Casterbridge to confess to his crime.

Bathsheba ordered the body to be removed to her house, and by herself she washed and dressed her dead husband for burial. But when the doctor, the vicar and Gabriel arrived, and she no longer needed to be strong, her self-control finally broke, and she became very ill. On the doctor's advice she was put to bed, and her illness continued for several months.

At his trial the following March Boldwood was found guilty of murder, for which the usual punishment was death. However, Weatherbury people began to protest publicly that he should not be held responsible for the crime. Over the last few weeks the villagers had noticed how his moods changed from wild despair to feverish excitement. He had forgotten his farm and even lost the previous year's harvest. And a pile of carefully wrapped parcels of dresses and jewels was found at his house, addressed to 'Bathsheba Boldwood' and dated six years ahead. These were accepted by the judges as signs of his madness, and in the end Boldwood was sent to prison for life. Gabriel knew that Bathsheba blamed herself for Troy's death, and would have blamed herself even more for Boldwood's.

Her health improved only very slowly. She hardly ever went out of the house or garden, and did not discuss her feelings with anyone, even Liddy. But by the summer she was beginning to spend more time in the open air, and one August evening she walked to the churchyard. She could hear the village children inside the church practising their singing for Sunday. She went straight to Fanny's grave, and read Troy's words on the large gravestone:

This stone was put up by Francis Troy in loving memory of Fanny Robin, who died on October 9, 1866, aged 20

Underneath, on the same stone, were the words she had added:

In the same grave lies Francis Troy who died on December 24, 1867, aged 26

As she listened to the sweet voices of the children coming from the church, and thought of the pain she had experienced in her short life, tears came to her eyes. She wished she were as innocent as those children again. She was still crying when she suddenly noticed Gabriel Oak, who had come up the path on his way to the church, and was watching her sympathetically.

'Are you going in?' she asked, trying to dry her tears.

'I *was*,' he replied. 'I'm one of the church singers, you know, and tonight's my practice evening. But I don't think I'll go in now.' There was a pause, while they both tried to think of something to say. At last Gabriel said slowly, 'I haven't seen you, to speak to, for a long time. Are you better now?'

'Yes, I am,' she replied. 'I came to look at the gravestone.'

'Eight months ago it happened!' said Gabriel. 'It seems like yesterday to me.'

'And to me it seems like years, long years ago.'

'There's something I must tell you,' said Gabriel, hesitating. 'The fact is, I won't be your farm manager much longer. I'm thinking of leaving England, and farming in America.'

There was a pause, while they both tried to think of something to say.

'Leaving England!' she cried in surprise and disappointment. 'But everyone thought you would rent poor Mr Boldwood's farm and manage it yourself!'

'The lawyers have offered it to me, it's true. But I'll be leaving Weatherbury next spring. I have my reasons.'

'And what shall I do without you? Oh Gabriel, we're such old friends! You've helped me so much in the past, and now that I'm more helpless than ever, you're going away!'

'It's unfortunate,' said Gabriel unhappily. 'It's *because* of that helplessness that I have to go,' and he walked so quickly out of the churchyard that she could not follow him.

In the next few months Bathsheba noticed miserably that Gabriel communicated with her as little as possible, and then only by messenger. She could not avoid thinking that he, the last friend she had, had lost interest in supporting her, and was about to desert her. On the day after Christmas she received the letter from him which she had been expecting. In it he explained that he would leave the farm in three months' time.

Bathsheba sat and cried bitterly over this letter. She was deeply hurt that Gabriel no longer loved her. She was also worried about having to manage the farm by herself again. She thought about it all morning, and was so depressed by the afternoon that she put on her cloak and found her way to where Gabriel lived. She knocked at the door.

'Who is it?' said Gabriel, opening the door. 'Oh, it's you, mistress!'

'I won't be your mistress much longer, will I, Gabriel?' she said sadly.

'Well, no, I suppose not.'

Because these two people, who knew each other well, were meeting in a strange place, they felt like the strangers they were when they first met, and neither spoke for a moment.

'Gabriel, perhaps I shouldn't have come, but I – I thought I must have offended you, and that's why you're going away.'

'Offended me! You couldn't do that, Bathsheba!'

'Couldn't I?' she said gladly. 'But then why are you going?'

'I'm not going to America, you know. I decided not to, when you seemed against the idea. No, I've arranged to rent Mr Boldwood's farm, and I could have been your farm manager as well, if – well – if people hadn't said things about us.'

'What?' said Bathsheba, surprised. 'What things?'

'Well, if you must know, that I'm just waiting and hoping for the chance to marry you some day.'

'Marry me! That's too foolish – too soon – to think of!'

'Yes, of course, it's foolish. I certainly agree.'

' "Too soon" were the words I used.'

'I'm sorry, but I think you said "too foolish".'

'I'm sorry too,' she replied with tears in her eyes. ' "Too soon" was what I said. But it doesn't matter a bit, not at all – but I only meant "too soon". Indeed, you must believe me!'

Gabriel looked into her face for a long time. 'Bathsheba,' he said, coming closer, 'If I only knew one thing – whether you'd allow me to love you, and marry you after all – if I only knew!'

'But you never will know,' she whispered.

'Why not?'

'Because you never ask.'

'Oh!' said Gabriel delightedly. 'My darling —'

'You should never have sent me that cruel letter this morning. It shows you don't care a bit about me!'

'Now Bathsheba,' he said, laughing, 'you know very well that I had to be very careful, as a single man working for you, a good-looking young woman. I've been so worried about your good name. That's why I was going to leave.'

'And that's the only reason? Oh, I'm so glad I came!' she cried thankfully, as she got up to leave. 'I've thought so much more about you since I imagined you didn't even want to see me again. But Gabriel, I shouldn't have come to visit you! *I* seem to be courting *you*! How awful!'

'Well, I've courted you, my beautiful Bathsheba, for a very long time, so one visit from you isn't much to ask.'

As he walked back to the farmhouse with her, they talked of his plans for Boldwood's farm. They spoke very little of their feelings for each other. They were such old friends that expressions of love were probably unnecessary. Their shared interests and their long, friendly relationship had given them a complete understanding of each other's character, and this finally developed, after their wedding, into a love that nothing could destroy.

A love that nothing could destroy . . .

GLOSSARY

admire to look at with pleasure, to like
barn a large farm building where hay, straw, etc. are kept
Bible the holy book of the Christian religion
blush *(v and n)* to become red in the face
brandy a strong alcoholic drink
cart an open wagon pulled by one or more horses
chalk-pit a deep hole where chalk has been dug
churchyard ground near a church where dead people are buried
circus a travelling show of animals and performers
cloak a coat without sleeves, which fastens at the neck and hangs
　loosely from the shoulders
clover a small green plant, grown as food for cattle, etc. (eating
　too much of it can be dangerous for sheep)
coffin a long box in which a dead person is placed before burial
court *(v)* to try to win a woman's love, with the idea of marrying
　her (not used today)
curl *(n)* a piece of hair growing in a round shape
darling a word used for someone who is much loved
despair *(n)* a feeling of hopelessness
drunk *(adj)* feeling the effects of too much alcoholic drink
fair *(n)* a country market where farm animals and products are
　bought and sold, farm workers are hired, etc.
flash to shine with a quick, bright light
flute a musical instrument played with the mouth and fingers
harvest to cut and gather wheat, hay, etc.
hay cut and dried grass, used as food for horses and cattle
hollow *(n)* a large hole or dip in the ground
hut a very small, simple building or shelter

improve to become better, or to make something better

lamb a young sheep

ma'am short for madam

maid a girl or woman servant

malthouse a building where malt (used in beer) is made; (in this story) a place where villagers meet to drink and talk

maltster a person who makes malt

mistress a woman who employs other people

nobleman a man from a family with a high social position

pity *(n)* a sympathetic understanding of another person's unhappiness

pregnant expecting a baby

pride being proud

propose (marriage) to suggest or offer marriage to someone

race a competition between horses, runners, etc. to see which is the fastest

relationship a feeling or situation connecting two people

respect to admire or have a high opinion of someone

respectable of good social position and good behaviour

rick a large pile of hay, wheat, etc., built in a regular shape

seal *(n)* a piece of melted wax, often stamped with words or a design, on an envelope to prevent it being opened

seal *(v)* to close an envelope with melted wax

shear to cut the wool off a sheep

shears a large cutting tool, shaped like scissors

shepherd a man who looks after sheep

spur *(n)* a sharp metal point worn on the heel of a rider's boot, used for making a horse go faster

stove a heater

straw the cut and dried stems of wheat, used for thatching, for animals to sleep on, etc.

strike *(v)* (of a clock) to indicate the time by sounding a bell

swollen grown bigger, wider, etc. than usual

sword a long sharp weapon used by soldiers

thatch *(v)* to make a roof for houses or ricks with straw

thoughtless not thinking of other people's feelings

toll money paid for the use of a road

toll-gate a gate across a road which is opened when the toll has been paid

trust *(v)* to have confidence in someone

vain too proud; having too high an opinion of one's appearance

valentine an unsigned card, expressing love, sent to arrive on St Valentine's day, 14th February

vicar a priest in the Church of England

wheat a plant which is harvested and used to make bread

workhouse in former times, a place provided by the government for the very poor, where they were fed and housed in exchange for work done

Far from the Madding Crowd

ACTIVITIES

Before Reading

1 The title of this book is *Far from the Madding Crowd*. What do you think it means?

   1 A place where there are no mad people

   2 A quiet, peaceful place anywhere

   3 A long way from crowded towns and cities

   4 Somewhere not close enough to fashionable people

   5 A long journey to a sad, lonely place

2 Read the story introduction on the first page of the book, and the back cover. Which of these sentences do you think are correct?

   1 Bathsheba Everdene is beautiful, but poor.

   2 She has to marry, in order to keep her farm.

   3 She has a choice of three possible husbands.

   4 She marries for convenience, not for love.

   5 Her experience of love brings her great unhappiness.

3 What do you think will happen in this story? Choose some of these ideas.

   1 Bathsheba will marry Farmer Boldwood.

   2 She will marry Gabriel Oak.

   3 She will marry Sergeant Troy.

   4 The man she marries will kill one of the other men.

   5 She will decide she prefers another man to her husband.

   6 She will be disappointed, and never find true love.

   7 She will marry more than once in her life.

While Reading

Read Chapters 1 to 5. Are these sentences true (T) or false (F)? Rewrite the false sentences with the correct information.

1 Gabriel Oak owned a farm and two hundred and fifty sheep.
2 Gabriel thought the girl in the red jacket was lovely, but vain.
3 The girl nearly killed Gabriel in his shepherd's hut.
4 Bathsheba accepted Gabriel's offer of marriage, although she didn't love him.
5 Most of Gabriel's sheep were killed in the chalk-pit.
6 Bathsheba was grateful to Gabriel for saving her wheat and offered him employment as her farm manager.
7 Gabriel saw Fanny Robin on the night she ran away.
8 Sergeant Troy had promised to marry Fanny Robin.
9 At the weekly market Mr Boldwood always stared at Bathsheba.
10 The valentine was a joke, but Mr Boldwood took it seriously.

Read Chapters 6 to 10, and answer these questions.

1 How did Mr Boldwood find out who had sent the valentine?
2 Why didn't Sergeant Troy marry Fanny Robin?
3 Why didn't Bathsheba refuse Boldwood's proposal at once?
4 Why did Bathsheba get so angry with Gabriel?
5 What made Gabriel return to help save the lives of her sheep?
6 How did Bathsheba first meet Sergeant Troy?
7 Why did Bathsheba agree to meet Troy at a hill near her house?
8 What did Troy do that made Bathsheba blush, and then cry?
9 What did Gabriel do that made Bathsheba angry?

Before you read Chapter 11, can you guess what happens? Choose Y (yes) or N (no) for each of these ideas.

1 When Boldwood gets Bathsheba's letter, he kills himself. Y/N
2 Boldwood becomes angry and threatens to punish Troy. Y/N
3 Bathsheba learns about Troy's promises to Fanny Robin. Y/N
4 Gabriel tries to prevent Troy from marrying Bathsheba. Y/N
5 Bathsheba leaves home secretly, and goes to find Troy. Y/N

Read Chapters 11 and 12. Who said this to whom, and who or what were they talking about?

1 'A love as strong as death. A letter cannot change that feeling.'
2 'Must you go on reminding me of it?'
3 'I've been blaming you, but it's his fault.'
4 'We thought someone had stolen the horse and cart.'
5 'I suppose I ought. Indeed, I want to, but I cannot.'
6 'She must love you madly to give herself so completely to you!'
7 'Now take your money back! I don't want it!'
8 'My new position won't change that, and I'll be friendly with you all, just as before.'

Read Chapters 13 to 15. Choose the best question-word for these questions, and then answer them.

How / What / Where / Who / Why

1 ... did the hay- and wheat-ricks need to be thatched?
2 ... managed to thatch them during the storm?
3 ... didn't the farm workers help with the thatching?
4 ... did Boldwood forget to have his ricks covered?
5 ... was Fanny Robin planning to spend the night?
6 ... was hidden in the back of Troy's watch?

7 ... well did Troy say he knew Fanny's young man?
8 ... did Bathsheba see when she opened Fanny's coffin?

Before you read Chapters 16 and 17, how do you think the lives of these four characters will change? Make some guesses.

1 Sergeant Troy   3 Mr Boldwood
2 Bathsheba   4 Gabriel Oak

Read Chapters 16 to 18. Complete these sentences with the names of characters in the story.

1 _____ ordered the best possible gravestone for _____.
2 _____ asked _____ to fill in the hole in _____'s grave.
3 _____ was rescued from drowning by sailors.
4 _____ became the farm manager for both _____ and _____.
5 _____ returned to England as a circus horse-rider.
6 _____ asked _____ to promise to marry him in six years' time.
7 _____ asked _____'s advice on whether to give this promise.
8 At the Christmas party, when _____ cried out in fear, _____ took a gun and shot _____.

Before you read Chapter 19, can you imagine how the story might end? Think of answers to these questions.

1 Is Troy dead, or badly wounded, or only hurt a little?
2 What will happen to Mr Boldwood? Will he kill himself?
3 If Troy is not dead, will he and Bathsheba live together again?
4 If Troy is dead, will Bathsheba marry again? If so, who?

What would be *your* advice to Bathsheba at this point, and why? And how would you *like* the story to end?

After Reading

1 **Write a short paragraph about each of these characters, using the words and phrases which best describe them. (Some words might suit more than one character.)**

BATHSHEBA EVERDENE   GABRIEL OAK
FRANK TROY   WILLIAM BOLDWOOD

- foolish   • respectable   • a good friend
- wealthy   • thoughtless   • independent-minded
- selfish   • determined   • could not be trusted
- sensible   • hard-working   • very strong feelings
- vain   • trusting   • lived only for the present
- serious   • reasonable   • always gave honest opinions
- patient   • middle-aged   • interested in pretty girls

2 **What is your opinion of the characters in this story? Use the descriptions you have written to help you discuss these questions.**

1 Should Bathsheba have agreed to marry Gabriel at the beginning of the story? Would their marriage have been successful then? If not, why not?

2 Why would Bathsheba never have been happy with Troy, even if he had lived?

3 Was Bathsheba right to go on refusing Boldwood's proposals? Could they ever have been happy together? Why, or why not?

4 Which qualities do you think are the most important when choosing a husband or wife?

3 **When Bathsheba returned from Bath (see pages 51/52), what did she say to her maid Liddy? Complete their conversation.**

LIDDY: Oh, miss, we've all been so worried! Where have you been?

BATHSHEBA: _____

LIDDY: Call you ma'am? You mean you went to Bath and got
   married? Oh, miss, I mean, ma'am, who did you – is it . . . ?

BATHSHEBA: _____

LIDDY: Oh, I do hope he'll make you a good husband, I really do.

BATHSHEBA: _____

LIDDY: I'll *try* to say only good things about him, ma'am. But it's
   so sudden! Did you plan to marry him when you went to Bath?

BATHSHEBA: _____

LIDDY: But I don't understand. If you went there to break off your
   relationship, then why did you marry him?

BATHSHEBA: _____

LIDDY: Seen a more beautiful woman than you? Oh, ma'am, he
   was lying! He probably just said that to make you jealous!

BATHSHEBA: _____

LIDDY: So now he'll have to stop chasing other girls, won't he?

BATHSHEBA: _____

LIDDY: Well, he would say that, wouldn't he? But I hope it's true.
   Oh, dear. Poor Mr Boldwood is going to be so unhappy!

BATHSHEBA: _____

LIDDY: Afraid of him? Why?

BATHSHEBA: _____

LIDDY: But he won't fight now Mr Troy's your husband, surely?

BATHSHEBA: _____

LIDDY: Yes, that's true. Everybody knows he's madly in love with
   you. Oh ma'am, you do lead a complicated life!

4 Names are often important in Hardy's stories. Can you find out the answers to these questions? Why do you think Hardy used these names for his characters?

  1 Who was Bathsheba (in history), and what was she famous for?
  2 What is an 'oak', and what qualities does it have?
  3 What does 'frank' mean, and what would the opposite be?

5 Imagine that Bathsheba wrote her diary for the day she watched Troy's sword practice (see Chapter 10). Choose the best word for each gap and complete her diary entry.

I shouldn't have agreed to meet him alone, but somehow he _____ me. He is so _____! I went to the place he had told me about. It was a deep, round _____ in the ground, completely _____ from the house and the path. And there he was, in his wonderful red _____! I had to stand in front of him and not _____, while his shining sword _____ through the air all around me, but never _____ me. At first I was afraid he would _____ me, but he told me the sword was not at all _____. But suddenly, a _____ of my hair fell to the ground! He had cut it _____ without my realizing!

  Then he said he would kill an _____ on my dress, and in horror I _____ his sword coming towards my _____. I was sure that _____ time I would die, but I felt almost _____ that my death would be at *his* hands. When I opened my _____, and saw the _____ insect on the point of the sword, I _____ how close I'd been to_____. He confessed he'd _____ about the sharpness of his sword, and I felt so _____ I had to sit down. He put the curl of my hair in his _____, next to his heart, and bent down to kiss me on the _____! I could not _____ him, nor did I want to. I shall never _____ that kiss.

6 Here is a newspaper report of the shooting at Mr Boldwood's house.
  Put the sentences in the right order, and join them with these linking
  words to make a paragraph of five sentences.

although / and / but / since / that / when / who

1 The dead man was Sergeant Frank Troy, husband of Bathsheba
   Troy,

2 _____ Sergeant Troy unexpectedly arrived at the party,

3 _____ it now appears that he had been living abroad.

4 Yesterday evening a man was shot and killed at the Boldwood
   farm in Weatherbury,

5 _____ her husband was reported drowned over a year ago,

6 Local people arriving at the house for a Christmas party knew
   Sergeant Troy had been seen in Casterbridge that day,

7 _____ owns the Everdene farm in Weatherbury.

8 took down a gun from the wall and shot him.

9 _____ early this morning Farmer William Boldwood, aged 43,
   was arrested for the murder.

10 Mrs Troy seemed so frightened of him

11 _____ his wife had not yet been informed of his return.

12 Mrs Troy has believed herself to be a widow

13 _____ Mr Boldwood, wanting to protect her,

7 Do you think the title of this book is a good one? Use the words
  below, with other words, to invent some different titles. Which title
  do you prefer for this story? Why?

shepherd	love	patient	harvest	valentine
farmer	despair	foolish	sword	heartache
soldier	trust	vain	wheatfield	beauty

ABOUT THE AUTHOR

Thomas Hardy was born in 1840 in the village of Higher Bockhampton in Dorset, in the south of England. The old stories and customs of country life were an important part of his childhood and family background. His father, a stonemason, led the singing in the church choir, and gave his son both an interest in church architecture and a feeling for music. Hardy attended local schools until he was sixteen, then became the pupil of a Dorchester church architect. His mother encouraged him to continue his wider studies, so he went on reading Latin and Greek in the evenings.

At twenty-two, he went to London to work as an architect, and it was here that he started writing. He found that publishers did not want his poetry, so he turned to novels, and wrote one a year from 1871 to 1875. The most popular of these was *Far from the Madding Crowd*, published in 1874. Its success meant that he could not only give up architecture and concentrate on writing, but also afford to get married. In the next twenty years he wrote short stories, poems, and twelve more novels, including *The Trumpet Major*, *The Mayor of Casterbridge*, and *The Woodlanders*. These were received with great enthusiasm, but *Tess of the d'Urbervilles*, published in 1891, was criticized for its sad ending and its description of the cruel realities of life for poor country people. And when *Jude the Obscure* came out in 1896, readers were horrified, protesting strongly at the novel's misery, despair, and hopelessness.

After this attack on his work, Hardy gave up writing novels, and returned to his first love, poetry. In the next thirty years he published eight volumes of poems, which range over life and death, love and loss, age and youth, peace and war. His marriage had been in difficulties for some time, and when his wife died suddenly in 1912, he wrote some of his most moving poems, full of sadness and guilt at her death. In 1914 he married again, and lived quietly at his home in Dorset, where his wife, and their dog Wessex, tried to protect him from the many admirers who came to visit. He died in 1928, and his ashes were laid in Poets' Corner of Westminster Abbey, while his heart was buried in the grave of his first wife.

Most of Hardy's novels are set in Dorset, and describe farming techniques and country customs in careful, loving detail. Like many country people, Hardy was a fatalist, and believed that whatever happens in life must simply be accepted. He was also a realist, and described people, their situations and problems, as they really were. Today, his novels are admired for their great themes of love and tragedy, and their beautiful descriptions of the English countryside as it used to be. Many of the novels have been successfully filmed.

Henry James, another famous novelist, criticized *Far from the Madding Crowd* and wrote: 'the only things we believe in are the sheep and the dogs'. Few people, however, agree with him, and it is still Hardy's best-loved novel. It has less of the darkness found in the later novels. Things go wrong but are also put right; there is bitterness and despair but also the warmth of long friendship, flowering within the endless circle of springtime and harvest. Hardy was thirty-three when he wrote this novel, and said many years later that 'perhaps there is something in it that I could not have put there if I had been older'.

OXFORD BOOKWORMS LIBRARY

Classics • Crime & Mystery • Factfiles • Fantasy & Horror
Human Interest • Playscripts • Thriller & Adventure
True Stories • World Stories

The OXFORD BOOKWORMS LIBRARY provides enjoyable reading in English, with a wide range of classic and modern fiction, non-fiction, and plays. It includes original and adapted texts in seven carefully graded language stages, which take learners from beginner to advanced level. An overview is given on the next pages.

All Stage 1 titles are available as audio recordings, as well as over eighty other titles from Starter to Stage 6. All Starters and many titles at Stages 1 to 4 are specially recommended for younger learners. Every Bookworm is illustrated, and Starters and Factfiles have full-colour illustrations.

The OXFORD BOOKWORMS LIBRARY also offers extensive support. Each book contains an introduction to the story, notes about the author, a glossary, and activities. Additional resources include tests and worksheets, and answers for these and for the activities in the books. There is advice on running a class library, using audio recordings, and the many ways of using Oxford Bookworms in reading programmes. Resource materials are available on the website <www.oup.com/bookworms>.

The *Oxford Bookworms Collection* is a series for advanced learners. It consists of volumes of short stories by well-known authors, both classic and modern. Texts are not abridged or adapted in any way, but carefully selected to be accessible to the advanced student.

You can find details and a full list of titles in the *Oxford Bookworms Library Catalogue* and *Oxford English Language Teaching Catalogues*, and on the website <www.oup.com/bookworms>.

THE OXFORD BOOKWORMS LIBRARY
GRADING AND SAMPLE EXTRACTS

STARTER • 250 HEADWORDS

present simple – present continuous – imperative –
can/cannot, must – *going to* (future) – simple gerunds ...

Her phone is ringing – but where is it?

Sally gets out of bed and looks in her bag. No phone. She looks under the bed. No phone. Then she looks behind the door. There is her phone. Sally picks up her phone and answers it. *Sally's Phone*

STAGE 1 • 400 HEADWORDS

... past simple – coordination with *and, but, or* –
subordination with *before, after, when, because, so* ...

I knew him in Persia. He was a famous builder and I worked with him there. For a time I was his friend, but not for long. When he came to Paris, I came after him – I wanted to watch him. He was a very clever, very dangerous man. *The Phantom of the Opera*

STAGE 2 • 700 HEADWORDS

... present perfect – *will* (future) – *(don't) have to, must not, could* –
comparison of adjectives – simple *if* clauses – past continuous –
tag questions – *ask/tell* + infinitive ...

While I was writing these words in my diary, I decided what to do. I must try to escape. I shall try to get down the wall outside. The window is high above the ground, but I have to try. I shall take some of the gold with me – if I escape, perhaps it will be helpful later. *Dracula*

... *should, may* – present perfect continuous – *used to* – past perfect –
causative – relative clauses – indirect statements ...

Of course, it was most important that no one should see
Colin, Mary, or Dickon entering the secret garden. So Colin
gave orders to the gardeners that they must all keep away
from that part of the garden in future. *The Secret Garden*

STAGE 4 • 1400 HEADWORDS

... past perfect continuous – passive (simple forms) –
would conditional clauses – indirect questions –
relatives with *where/when* – gerunds after prepositions/phrases ...

I was glad. Now Hyde could not show his face to the world
again. If he did, every honest man in London would be proud
to report him to the police. *Dr Jekyll and Mr Hyde*

STAGE 5 • 1800 HEADWORDS

... future continuous – future perfect –
passive (modals, continuous forms) –
would have conditional clauses – modals + perfect infinitive ...

If he had spoken Estella's name, I would have hit him. I was so
angry with him, and so depressed about my future, that I could
not eat the breakfast. Instead I went straight to the old house.
Great Expectations

STAGE 6 • 2500 HEADWORDS

... passive (infinitives, gerunds) – advanced modal meanings –
clauses of concession, condition

When I stepped up to the piano, I was confident. It was as if I
knew that the prodigy side of me really did exist. And when I
started to play, I was so caught up in how lovely I looked that
I didn't worry how I would sound. *The Joy Luck Club*